Samuel W. Bloom

Social Functions
of
Medical Practice

Doctor-Patient Relationships
in Israel

Judith T. Shuval

In Collaboration with

Aaron Antonovsky

and

A. Michael Davies

SOCIAL
FUNCTIONS
OF
MEDICAL
PRACTICE

Jossey-Bass Inc., Publishers
615 Montgomery Street · San Francisco · 1970

SOCIAL FUNCTIONS OF MEDICAL PRACTICE
Doctor-Patient Relationships in Israel
By Judith T. Shuval in collaboration with
Aaron Antonovsky and A. Michael Davies

Jossey-Bass, Inc., Publishers
615 Montgomery Street
San Francisco, California 94111

Library of Congress Catalog Card Number 77–110633

International Standard Book Number ISBN 0–87589–068–7

Manufactured in the United States of America
Composed and printed by York Composition Company, Inc.
Bound by Chas. H. Bohn & Co., Inc.

JACKET DESIGN BY WILLI BAUM, SAN FRANCISCO

FIRST EDITION

Code 7017

THE JOSSEY-BASS BEHAVIORAL SCIENCE SERIES

General Editors

WILLIAM E. HENRY
University of Chicago

NEVITT SANFORD
Wright Institute, Berkeley

Special Adviser in Medical Sociology

ETHEL SHANAS
University of Illinois, Chicago Circle

Preface

There is growing awareness in many parts of the world of the need for mass delivery of medical care to broad population groups. Neither the solo practitioner nor the charity clinic can be viewed as the only arrangement for effective delivery of medical care to large numbers of people. The pattern coming increasingly to prevail is that of a sizeable clinic that deals with large numbers of patients on a prepayment, reimbursement, or publicly sponsored health insurance basis.

The growing trend to remove financial barriers or to rationalize payment systems for medical care and to shift practice from the private office to the modern clinic carries broad implications for the structure of the physician-patient relationship and for the quality of medical care. Complex medical care is reaching segments of the population that never before enjoyed such services. As ability to pay becomes less crucial in determining who will take advantage of available medical services, patterns of motivation become more central.

In some parts of the world, people with insufficient motivation, notably lower-class groups, underutilize medical services and may therefore obtain inadequate medical care. Likewise, overutilization may occur when people misunderstand the doctor's or the clinic's appropriate function. This could mean that some people are motivated to see their doctor by nonmedical needs, needs that might be satisfied in some other context. When overutilization of clinic facilities is extreme, the quality of medical care may be adversely affected: physicians who are under pressure to provide service to too many patients cannot invest the time and effort necessary to assure high-quality care.

The clinic relationship, unlike the relationship of the physician and his patient in a fee-for-service system, is more impersonal and bureaucratic. While in many cases this impersonality may result in some dissatisfaction by clients, it is still unclear what long-range results this impersonality may have for the quality of medical care.

A detailed study of the doctor-patient relationship under different systems of practice would go a long way to clarify these problems. *Social Functions of Medical Practice* sheds light on some of them within the context of one system of practice: the clinics of Kupat Holim, the largest medical institution in Israel. Certain unique features of this institution and of the population that utilizes it—and of the overall social context in which both operate—point up several theoretical and practical problems involved in the social system made up of the doctor and his patient.

Focusing on patients' motives and needs on the one hand and on physicians' attitudes and patterns of response on the other, this book may be able to provide some information on the restructuring of the physician-patient relationship and on several of its implications. The approach taken is essentially sociological, but, as noted, the substance of the problems dealt with should also be of interest to physicians and other health practitioners, since those problems are general enough that the implications of this book should be relevant in other settings as well.

Social Functions of Medical Practice could not have been undertaken without the wholehearted cooperation of Kupat Holim, the Sick Fund of the General Federation of Labor in Israel. We are especially indebted to Dr. Tova Yeshurun-Berman who, as Medical Director of Kupat Holim, was more that helpful in securing the participation of the district clinics in our research undertaking. Dr. Alexander Fleisher, who headed the Jerusalem District of Kupat Holim at the time the study was initiated, played an important role in obtaining the participation of the neighborhood clinics and physicians in the Jerusalem area. Izhak Kanev, Chairman of Kupat Holim and Director of the Histadrut's Economic and Research Institute, as well as N. Strubovitz of the Research and Statistics Department of Kupat Holim, were at all times most cooperative in providing hard-to-find information. To the hundreds of Kupat Holim members and physicians who willingly participated in the study we are immeasurably grateful.

It goes without saying that the research reported here was aimed at understanding the social structure of the doctor-patient relationship in terms of certain sociological concepts and did not have as its purpose an evaluation of the facilities and services of Kupat Holim. It is hoped, however, that certain of the findings will be of use in rethinking the many problems involved in delivery of medical care to broad population groups in many parts of the world.

Support for the research was first given by the Ford Foundation and subsequently by the Benjamin Rosenthal Foundation and by Grant RG-8187 of the National Institute of General Medical Sciences of the United States Department of Health, Education, and Welfare.

The study benefited greatly from the wealth of experience and excellent research facilities of the Israel Institute of Applied Social Research, under whose auspices the research was carried out. Many members of the technical, field, and professional staff participated in the study for varying periods of time. It is impossible to list them all but their competent and devoted assistance is deeply appreciated.

This research represents a collaborative effort. A. Michael Davies represented the medical profession and saw to it that the study did not lose its medical perspective. Aaron Antonovsky strengthened the social science viewpoint and helped formulate the research problem in its broader sociological perspective. Both served as enthusiastic and creative collaborators whose devotion and insight contributed markedly to the research effort.

Jerusalem   JUDITH T. SHUVAL
March 1970

Contents

Preface   ix

PART ONE: SETTING

1. Framework of the Study   3

2. Method and Field Procedures   31

3. Ethnic Groups   38

PART TWO: ATTITUDES

4. Kupat Holim: Patterns of Utilization   61

5. Defining Oneself as Ill   80

PART THREE: LATENT FUNCTIONS

6. Setting for Catharsis   91

7. Coping with Failure   110

8. Integration into Israel   127

9. Gaining Status   144

10. Magic-Science Conflict   161

PART FOUR: CLOSING

11. Social Functions of Medical Practice   181

Bibliography   201

Selected Ethnic Bibliography   212

Index   217

Social Functions
of
Medical Practice

Doctor-Patient Relationships
in Israel

PART ONE

SETTING

1

Framework of the Study

The theoretical focus of this study is on certain latent functions of the medical institution for its clients. Merton (1949) has defined the manifest functions of an institution as "those objective consequences contributing to the adjustment or adaptation of the system which are intended and recognized by participants in the system." In the case of Kupat Holim, the medical institution under consideration here, these manifest functions can be defined as the practice of curative and preventive medicine. Latent functions are those consequences "which are neither intended nor recognized" (p. 51).

When clients feel that these latent functions are desirable, they may be what motivates them to use the institution's facilities. Clients may be motivated to "enjoy" both the manifest and the latent functions of an institution. Because patients are likely to rationalize attendance at a clinic in terms of illness and the need for medical care does not mean that there are no other goals in their motivation (Rosenstock, 1966).

In Israel, clinic attendance is among the highest in the world (see Chapter Four). This high utilization rate might be accounted for, at least in part, by clients seeking to "enjoy" latent functions of the medical institution in addition to its manifest ones, because morbidity rates alone are too low to account for such frequent utilization. The explanation therefore could lie in the nature of the client population, in the social structure of the medical institution, in the social system of the larger society, and in the interaction among them. One of the goals of this study is to shed some light on these variables and on their interrelationships.

The latent functions of the medical institution stem from certain of its structural features, from the professional role of the physician, and from the nature of the sick role. Each of these is affected by the social context of Israeli society, which serves to point up special aspects of these latent functions.

Another area of interest that motivated this research is immigrant adjustment and acculturation. The medical institution under study is markedly Western in its value orientation, occupies a central position in Israeli society, and can be said to represent many of the dominant values of that society. By concentrating on one specific social institution, the study attempts to focus on immigrants' adaptation to it. In recent years, contact between immigrants and host societies has been mediated by professionals and bureaucrats—customs officials, social workers, public health nurses, housing administrators and, in the present case, physicians (Katz and Eisenstadt, 1960).

Interest in the acculturation problem determined the client population to be studied: we deliberately chose ethnic groups of immigrants with varying backgrounds of experience with Western-oriented medicine and with a bureaucratic structure of medical service. The groups chosen were Jewish immigrants from Kurdistan, Morocco, Rumania, and Poland who arrived in Israel after the establishment of the state in 1948. This choice was dictated by the fact that prior to immigration to Israel, the Kurdish subjects had a minimum of contact with Western-oriented medical institutions, the Moroccans had somewhat more, while the Rumanians and Poles, who immigrated from behind the Iron Curtain, had had, comparatively speaking, a maximum of experience with such institutions and values (see Chapter Three).

This combination of interests led to the formulation of the research problem. Basically the study is concerned with patients' attempts to "enjoy" certain latent functions of the medical institution. The motivation for such efforts could be associated with needs stemming from the acculturation process. Whether patients succeed or fail to satisfy such needs through the institution depends in large part on patterns of physician response. Doctors may be unaware, unable, or unwilling to perform their professional role in such a way as to satisfy these clients' needs. The study is therefore concerned with mutual sets of expectations of physicians and patients and with the extent of their congruence.

The problem of high clinic utilization ties in systematically with this formulation. One way of looking at high utilization is in terms of unfulfilled expectations of clients. If patients are repeatedly seeking satisfaction of a need through one of the latent functions of the institution, while the physician, for whatever reason, is failing to provide such satisfaction, a ritualistic pattern of attendance may result: patients repeatedly seek satisfaction of a need through the institution. If, on the other hand, physicians do satisfy the need, patients will be motivated to "enjoy" the latent functions of the institution. In both cases high rates of utilization would result.[1]

Such an approach does not mean that there are no other possible factors that could be causing high clinic utilization. This study does not touch systematically on the numerous dysfunctions of bureaucratic medicine which often result in patients being sent from doctor to doctor or from laboratory to laboratory, by physicians who are unable—or unwilling—to assume full responsibility for decision-making. Research examining these problems requires a design rather different from the present undertaking.

We have not attempted to propose an exhaustive list of the possible latent functions of the medical institution, but have chosen to focus only on five latent functions that appear to be central to

[1] For a discussion of some of these issues in Britain, see Browne and Freeling, 1965; Simon, 1966.

the institution and of considerable substantive interest as well. These five latent functions are considered in the light of the needs they satisfy. These needs are: (1) the need for catharsis; (2) the need to cope with failure; (3) the need for integration into Israeli society; (4) the need for status; and (5) the need for resolution of a magic-science conflict.

The full implications of these latent functions can best be seen by considering four general areas: (1) the character and place of the specific medical institution in the context of Israeli social structure; (2) certain sociological components of the sick role; (3) certain sociological components of the physician's role; and (4) the nature of the immigrant populations and their needs.

KUPAT HOLIM

The Kupat Holim ("sick fund") is the medical arm of the Histadrut, the General Federation of Labor, and is the most powerful medical institution in Israel. Most employed persons in Israel are organized in the Histadrut. Monthly union dues entitle them to membership in Kupat Holim. In addition many self-employed persons belong to the Histadrut in order to obtain medical care.

Such membership entitles members and their dependents to comprehensive medical care, hospitalization, and free or reduced-cost medicines. Orthopedic appliances, dental care, and prostheses are supplied at cost price. Members are entitled to free use of convalescent homes after serious illness or hospitalization (Grushka, 1968).

New immigrants may receive medical care from Kupat Holim, paid for by the Jewish Agency, for the first three months after arrival; recipients of relief benefits may be cared for under a similar arrangement with the Department of Social Welfare. A Kupat Holim clinic is often the first institution to be erected in a new immigrant village or housing estate. Factory doctors are usually provided by Kupat Holim and in many areas, mainly in communal settlements, preventive services for mothers and children come from the same source. Thus, for a majority of Israel's inhabitants, Kupat Holim is *the* medical institution and the primary source of medical care. Indeed, "going to Kupat Holim" has come to be virtually synonymous in Israel with "going to the doctor."

Some of the statistics on Kupat Holim indicate the dominant role it plays in Israel's medical services. In 1966 the Fund employed nearly 14,000 persons, of whom 2,685 were physicians and 4,266 nurses. It maintained 3,187 beds in fourteen general and special hospitals, manned 1,021 clinics and 180 mother and child care stations, and gave health supervision to 249 schools and educational establishments (Kupat Holim, 1967). At its own expense, Kupat Holim also enables its members to utilize hospitals and other medical facilities run by other institutions. The Kupat Holim budget for 1966–1967 was 287 million pounds ($95.7 million) compared to 151 million pounds ($50.3 million) for the Ministry of Health.

At the time of the study, Kupat Holim was providing medical care for 1,905,000 persons (members and their dependents), constituting 71.7 per cent of the Jewish population. The other five smaller sick funds, together, accounted for 18.7 per cent, leaving less than 10 per cent not covered by health insurance (Israel Central Bureau of Statistics, 1967). While there is no compulsory health insurance in Israel, it can be seen that the overwhelming majority of the population is insured.

Kupat Holim concentrates its services on acute medical conditions and on ambulatory care in clinics, particularly in the smaller towns and rural areas. It is also active in the areas of mother and child care, medical services in educational institutions, and in the areas of chronic disease and rehabilitation, although the Ministry of Health, municipalities, and voluntary agencies play a comparatively more active role in these areas.

Physicians are paid a salary according to a national wage scale and only a few have permission to engage in private practice. General practitioners, who comprise over half of the doctors employed by Kupat Holim, are paid a full salary for the care of 1,400 members in an urban area and for 850 members in a rural area, during an eight-hour day. Should the local situation require a physician to care for a larger number, his salary is increased proportionately. Physicians over fifty-five are entitled to reduce their hours of work. For a seven-hour day the total patient load is 1,225, and 1,050 for a six-hour day (Kupat Holim, 1964b).

Most of the direct ambulatory services are given in clinics erected by Kupat Holim and these take the place of the doctor's

office. Members of Kupat Holim are registered with a particular
clinic and often with a particular doctor. When they wish to see
the doctor they report to clinic early in the morning or in the after-
noon, depending on the clinic hours. In larger clinics, in which
several physicians work, patients are given a numbered ticket by the
clerk. The number determines their places in the line and the clerk
limits attendance by an official "norm," laid down by the medical
directorate of Kupat Holim, which fixes the maximum number of
patients that can be seen by each physician at four to six an hour.
The clerk may admit extra patients out of line if the urgency of
their cases warrants this (Kupat Holim, 1964b, p. 21). Few attempts have been made to institute an appointments system and it
is not unusual for patients to wait several hours to see the doctor.
The norm of four to six patients an hour cannot always be kept
owing to the pressure of patients. In a survey of four large urban
clinics in 1964, 55 per cent of the doctors saw up to five and one
half patients each hour, while 31 per cent were seeing more than
six (Kupat Holim, 1964b, p. 8). Thus the clerk plays a key role in
deciding who shall see the doctor.

  Clinics are usually located in local communities or neighborhoods. This means that there is almost always a Kupat Holim
clinic within close range of all members. Members are not limited in
the number of visits they may make to see the physician. Access to the
doctor is therefore limited only by the patient's willingness to get
to the clinic early and wait his turn. This relatively easy and convenient accessibility to the clinic physician is a central factor in the
formulation of our hypotheses.

  The association of the medical profession with science and
research combine to give it a certain aura of prestige. Israeli society
accords a high measure of esteem to scientific endeavors and to the
institutional structures in which they are carried out. Kupat Holim,
while concerned mainly with applied science rather than research,
may nevertheless be said to operate within a scientific set of values;
it is thus probably accorded a measure of the prestige associated
with science. The physical trappings of the clinic—white coats,
pharmaceuticals, elaborate medical equipment—emphasize its scientific nature. So do the many tests to which patients are frequently
subjected.

No systematic study has been carried out on the comparative prestige of various occupations in Israel but it is our impression that, despite differences among various specialties, the medical profession as a whole enjoys relatively high status. This high prestige may be partly explained by the relatively long period of formal training required by the profession. Another factor could be the emphasis on and importance of health in Israeli society. European Jews are notoriously concerned with their own and their families' health problems and this concern may have contributed to the central place that health occupies in the value system (Zborowski and Herzog, 1952, p. 354). Furthermore medicine has traditionally occupied a high status position in many of the countries from which immigrants came and they may have transferred an attitude of respect and deference to the profession in Israel, thus retaining its image as a high status occupation.

Kupat Holim is an integral part of the Histadrut, the General Federation of Labor. Founded in 1912, it has come to occupy a central place among the many activities of the Histadrut. Membership in the Federation of Labor has always carried the privilege of Kupat Holim membership (Grushka, 1968, p. 180). Association with the Histadrut, which for many years has occupied a central and dominant position in the Jewish community, has projected an image of Kupat Holim as an integral and representative institution in the society. We have already noted that for the vast majority of the population it is *the* medical institution in the country and has come to represent many of the socialist and humanitarian values which have been so prominent in Israeli society.

The characteristics of Kupat Holim which are most salient for our analysis are: (1) broad coverage of the population; (2) prepaid comprehensive medical care for members; (3) easy accessibility of the physician to members; (4) relatively high status of the institution and its physician personnel in the society; and (5) representativeness of the institution in terms of the central value system of the society.

SICK ROLE

Parsons' (1951) analysis of the sick role emphasizes the dependency and regressiveness inherent in it and the patient's lack of obligation to carry out his usual tasks and obligations. He has further noted the "voluntaristic" element in illness (see also Gordon, 1966). Clearly for some people there may be latent rewards in illness itself as well as in the medical institution that deals with illness.

The sick role involves a greater measure of passivity than is generally acceptable in other roles in an active value context. The patient is not required to take an active role in carrying out his usual responsibilities. Furthermore, he is required to accept, passively and submissively, instructions, medicines, and other forms of treatment administered by professional personnel or members of his family. Regressiveness is expressed in passive acceptance of authority. Thus the sick role involves passivity, not only from the point of view of abrogating responsibilities, but also in terms of the patient's orientation toward those caring for him.

Parsons (1951) notes that the patient has the obligation to want to get well and is supposed to cooperate with the physician with this aim in view (p. 437). This is particularly true in a society in which an active frame of reference provides a dominant value orientation. In such situations the passivity involved in illness may be guilt-producing: people are likely to resent illness and may strive to move out of the role. However, for people with a basically passive value orientation, the passivity of the sick role would tend to complement their general orientation.

Another way in which the sick role may be rewarding is in helping the individual cope with failure to carry out certain role obligations. Berle (1958) has stated that ". . . illness may be an aspect of lack of success and may therefore become a justification for failure. Failure is almost inevitable when there is a discrepancy between an individual's aspirations and the limited opportunities opened to him. To prove illness, so that one may be cared for, is then a vital necessity" (p. 206). From this point of view, being sick explains and justifies failure. The individual argues, either to himself or to others, that he cannot succeed because he is not well enough to function to his full capacity. From this point of view the sick role may be rewarding. Again, this will be less true in an actively oriented culture in which illness may be guilt-producing.

In addition the sick role may provide leverage to gain certain other rewards. These include admission to an institution in order to get others to undertake care of one's daily needs. In Israel it may also entitle one to such benefits as easier work conditions or better housing. In this sense the sick role is potentially rewarding particularly to people who are unable to attain such goals by other means (Moses and Hoek, 1961).

The crucial points to be noted about the sick role are: its passive orientation which may provide latent rewards to certain types of individuals, particularly those from cultural backgrounds emphasizing passive value orientations; and its potential for helping people cope with failure to perform social roles adequately.

PHYSICIAN'S ROLE

In Western society the physician is the only person recognized as the legitimizer of illness. It is not enough for the individual to claim to be sick: before entering the sick role it is necessary to obtain "official" recognition that one is indeed ill. We may assume that the attractions of the latent rewards inherent in illness as well as society's need for social control in order to prevent large-scale deviance in the form of avoidance of social responsibility have brought about the need for expert, professional legitimation (Parsons, 1951).

A document attesting to a legitimized illness is known in Israel as a *petek*, literally a note. There are a remarkable number of situations requiring such formal certification of illness by the doctor: absence from work, obtaining housing privileges, eligibility for less strenuous forms of work, social welfare benefits, relocation of residence to a different part of the country when public housing is needed, and many others (Moses and Hoek, 1961). In a society in which rewards of this sort are often scarce, particularly for immigrants, sickness may be an attractive mechanism to attain them. The humanely oriented doctor is under pressure to accede to requests for a petek, particularly when they come from hard-pressed immigrants.

Ideally, the physician's orientation toward his patient is permissive and supportive. Without pushing the analogy of the psychiatrist too far, it may be said that the general practitioner's role requires general acceptance and an uncritical attitude toward patients. Even with respect to vague and ambiguous symptoms without objective signs, such as headaches, stomachaches, back-aches, the professional role of the physician pressures him to be ac-cepting and to avoid excessive criticism. Disregard of such ambigu-ous symptoms could result in misdiagnosis.

Furthermore contemporary medicine has come increasingly to accept the relevance of the broader aspects of the patient's life to his illness: his family relations, his work situation, his place in the community. Although awareness of the importance of this broad orientation may not yet exist among all general practitioners, there is a growing concern with it. What this means is that increasingly the physician must consider and take into account a wide range of problems, some of them possibly marginal to the specific ailment.

These elements in the physician's role open him to potential "exploitation" by patients. The professional risk of making a mis-take is great enough to prevent the conscientious physician from taking a rigid, critical stand. A suspected malingerer might be ill, and the patient's ramblings might provide a clue to diagnosis. This is not to say that all physicians are conscientious or that they always behave in a supportive, uncritical manner in the face of pressure by patients. But unless they have been systematically frustrated, patients have reason to expect professional role performance more or less along the lines described.

The physician's orientation toward his patient is ideally universalistic. He is concerned only with the individual as a patient and relates to him in terms of norms clearly defined by the profes-sion. He should have no interest in the impingement of other roles or characteristics. He should not, for example, take account of the patient's ethnic or class background, except as these are directly relevant to the patient's illness. This ideal of the profession is not always carried out, but it remains a fundamental norm of the pro-fessional role.

The bureaucratic structure tends to reinforce the universal-istic norm of the medical profession. A universalistic orientation toward clients is a *sine qua non* of a properly functioning bureauc-racy. Unambiguous rules define eligibility for service as well as obligations and norms of bureaucratic personnel in providing such service. This is further reinforced by the equalitarian ethic of the Histadrut.

The ethic of the medical profession combines with the bureaucratic norm to pressure the Kupat Holim physician toward adherence to a universalistic orientation to clients. Deviation from such a pattern involves a break with two sets of norms. Thus the pressure on the Kupat Holim physician to maintain a universalistic orientation is greater than it is for the solo practitioner or for a non-professional bureaucrat.

In sum, the crucial points to be noted about the physician's role are: his position as sole legitimizer of illness exposes him to exploitation by patients who are utilizing illness to gain certain latent rewards; the requirement of a permissive, supportive, uncritical orientation toward patients exposes the physician to potential exploitation by patients with a need to unburden themselves; and both the professional ethic and the bureaucratic structure pressure the physician toward a universalistic orientation toward patients.

NEEDS OF IMMIGRANT POPULATIONS

In his example of the latent functions of the political machine, Merton (1949) notes that the institution serves certain needs of the population. He states, for example, that the institution satisfies an economic need of the "deprived classes" for personal, humanitarian, rather than bureaucratic, assistance in the form of food baskets or settling scrapes with the law. It also satisfies the need for special political privileges of the business interests and the need for social mobility among those to whom legitimate channels are less open. Our study follows Merton's approach in proposing an association between a number of needs of the population and certain latent functions of the medical institution (Bredemeier, 1955).

While such needs may be said to exist to some extent in all populations, there is good reason to suppose that they are particularly felt by immigrants. Indeed, it will be seen that several of them are associated directly with problems of transition into a new social system.

It should be noted that the needs studied are not the only ones pressing on these populations. We have selected them not only for their substantive interest, but because of their complementarity to the latent functions of the medical institution.

Catharsis. Immigration brings in its wake certain dislocations in primary relationships, particularly for groups that previously lived within the framework of extended family systems. Immigration almost always results in a disruption of existing networks of relationships and in sudden detachment from at least some affective ties (Weinberg, 1961). In recent years, more than in the earliest years of the state, settlement authorities have consciously attempted not to break up such networks and to retain ethnic subgroups in a residential context whenever feasible. Even so, it would seem that those groups for whom family ties were especially important, would feel the strain of isolation in the new social context. While this problem would probably apply mostly to North African and Near Eastern immigrants who are likely to have lived within traditional family structures in their countries of origin, the strain of detachment and isolation exists among many European immigrants as well.

The feeling of isolation and detachment among immigrants is reinforced by language barriers as well as by the difficulties of communication resulting from wide cultural differences. Despite recent attempts to settle members of ethnic groups together, those living in larger communities or development towns of necessity find themselves surrounded by immigrants from other countries. This cultural heterogeneity, combined with status differentials that emerge over time, often results in relatively little social contact even between groups living in close propinquity.

Intergenerational conflict often sets up barriers even within nuclear family structures. Parents can no longer adequately serve as role models for their children in a situation of transition where the cultural gap between the generations is large. Traditional patterns of behavior are no longer acceptable to the younger, more acculturated generation, while the more Western-oriented patterns of the young people meet with disdain or hostility from their elders. Communication may therefore be poor, not only between ethnic groups, but often between members of the same nuclear family.

Many traditional cultures provide specialists to whom individuals may turn for advice when they have a problem. Such specialists often provide a sympathetic, permissive, supportive context in which the troubled person can talk freely and confidentially. The priest, rabbi, or "wise woman" often filled this role (Roemer,

1963). In the Israeli context such specialists may not be practicing any longer or may have lost much of the confidence of their clients as a result of the impingement of a Western value system which tends to disparage their effectiveness.

Against this background it would seem that many immigrants might have a real need for the kind of social contact that permits or encourages free communication. There may be a need among some immigrants for a sympathetic ear lent in an uncritical, supportive atmosphere. One place in which such a supportive listener can be relatively easily gained is in the Kupat Holim clinic, where the doctor's professional role presumably requires him to behave in a manner that will satisfy this need. When the immigration process has limited other possible loci to satisfy this need, the easily accessible Kupat Holim physician may play a critical role in satisfying it.[2]

Coping with Failure. The problem of failure is especially relevant to immigrants and they may therefore be likely to utilize illness as a means of coping with it. The dislocation inherent in transition to a new society is conducive to a feeling of failure. Not only are there objective, physical obstacles to be overcome, but aspirations are not always realized, especially in the early stages of settlement (Shuval, 1963). Feelings of relative deprivation and selective retrospective recall of conditions in their countries of origin could cause immigrants to feel that their present performance and achievements are not fully up to standard.

We have already noted that there are several ways in which illness can act as a means of coping with failure. An individual can rationalize his failure by pleading illness as an acceptable reason for not being able to perform. Illness can legitimize institutionalization in a hospital or other custodial establishment, thus taking the burden of performance off the failing individual and shifting it to others. Finally, illness, in Israeli society, often makes possible the attainment of rewards in the areas of housing, employment conditions, and social welfare that some people are unable to attain by the usual channels. While other mechanisms for coping with failure exist, these may often be less attractive than illness.

[2] For a study in which limited alternatives have apparently motivated doctor attendance, see Stoekle and Davidson, 1963.

Since illness requires legitimation by the physician, members of Kupat Holim characterized by a feeling of failure may be especially likely to visit the doctor in an attempt to gain such legitimation (Berle, 1958, p. 206).

Integration into Israeli Society. The process of integration into Israeli society requires that immigrants gradually shed their ethnic identity and gain a new one until they are identifiable as Israelis rather than as immigrants from a specific country of origin. The process of losing one's ethnic identity is a slow one which can take years or even generations. This is true even in the case of a Jew migrating to a Jewish country.

The need to become integrated into Israeli society is differentially distributed among immigrants: some are more tenaciously attached to their ethnic groups than others. What is perhaps more important is the fact that opportunities to satisfy such a need, that is, to shed one's ethnic identity, are not available to all on an equal basis. Partly this is because expressions of prejudice in the society, directed primarily at non-Europeans, tend to reinforce and heighten the visibility and identifiability of non-Europeans, thus making it more difficult for them to shed their ethnic identification and become Israelis (Shuval, 1956; 1962a). Situations that minimize the relevance of an individual's ethnic origin would seem to be especially suited to the satisfaction of this need, since in such contexts the individual can build up a set of relations based on criteria other than his ethnic membership.

It would seem that Kupat Holim, with its strong pressures toward universalistic orientations to patients, could serve as such a context. While there may be other contexts in the society that serve this purpose, the availability and accessibility of Kupat Holim might make it a particularly attractive locus to satisfy this need, especially among non-European immigrants to whom alternative contexts may be somewhat less readily available.

Status. Immigration often results in a measure of occupational dislocation as a result of differences in economic and occupational structure between the countries of origin and the host country (Hanoch, 1961; Matras, 1965; Shuval, 1963). Frequently occupational adjustment involves a move downward in status, at least for some period of adaptation, and in some cases there may be need for radical occupational relocation. In cases where there has been a loss of status through such relocation, the result may be a high level of status-sensitivity and a need to gain status whenever the occasion presents itself.

Immigrants to Israel from North African and Near Eastern countries generally enter the social system at a comparatively low status level, owing to their relatively poor educational background and the unskilled occupations in which many of them were employed before immigration. Although Israeli society is a comparatively open one and many upwardly mobile immigrants have succeeded in moving out of this impasse, inadequate education as well as a more passive value orientation have combined to slow down the upward mobility of many members of such groups (Hanoch, 1961; Lissak, 1969; Matras, 1965; Shuval, 1963).

The opportunities for status attainment are relatively limited for low-ranking groups and particularly for those of North African and Near Eastern origin. While the lack of opportunity may be no worse than in many other societies, the contrast between equalitarian norms and realistic opportunities could induce an exaggerated need for status among upwardly mobile groups (Merton, 1949). Furthermore, certain expressions of prejudice tend to limit other potential areas in which non-European immigrants can satisfy their need for status (Shuval, 1956, 1962a, 1962b, 1966). When alternative sources for need gratification are limited, the availability and accessibility of Kupat Holim—with its aura of prestige and status— could serve to satisfy this need.

Resolving Magic-Science Conflict. Immigrants from Near Eastern or North African countries sometimes made use of traditional medical practitioners in their countries of origin. Such traditional practitioners may still be used in Israel although normative pressures of a Western-oriented society tend to push them into the darker recesses of local neighborhoods. However, there is reason to assume that for certain types of illness, particularly those for which Western medicine cannot provide direct, clearly visible, efficacious remedies, some people may continue to seek out the services of traditional practitioners. To a more limited extent, this is probably true of Europeans as well.

Interestingly enough, 12 per cent of our total population of

Kupat Holim members stated openly that they themselves continue to use traditional medical practitioners in case of need. Among the rural non-Europeans as many as 20 per cent said this. Furthermore, 19 per cent of the total population and fully a third of the rural non-Europeans believe that such practitioners "definitely have a legitimate area of practice in Israel."

Use of traditional practitioners does not necessarily imply lack of confidence in, or failure to utilize, Western medical institutions. There may occur parallel utilization, either in terms of differentiation by types of illness treated in each context or even treatment for the same illness in both contexts. In any case, it is important to note that use of one type of practitioner does not eliminate the likelihood of use of the other.

The Western context of Israeli society, with its emphasis on rationality and science, conflicts in many ways with the subcultural contexts of traditionally oriented people. With the exception of certain limited reference groups, there would probably be a tendency in most circles to disvalue such traditional practices. People who make use of traditional medical practitioners would thus probably feel a certain discomfort, sensing that these practitioners are not quite up to the times in Israel. We are not suggesting that such conflict would completely inhibit traditional patterns, since seeking medical care of this sort probably involves fairly deep affective needs. It would seem, however, that use of traditional medical practitioners probably entails a certain disequilibrium and a need to resolve the value conflict aroused.

One way to help resolve such conflict is by demonstrating to oneself or to one's salient reference groups that one identifies wholeheartedly with the rational-scientific values of Israeli society. From this point of view, a strong, overt orientation to Western values would be functional in helping reduce such conflict. It is as though the individual were publicly proclaiming his acceptance of and identification with science rather than with traditional magic.

The need, as we have defined it here, is somewhat different from those previously discussed. We are speaking of a need to resolve conflict between values which condone use of traditional medical practitioners and Western-oriented values. The need is to reduce or eliminate the disequilibrium and discomfort inherent in such value conflict.

The Kupat Holim clinic provides one easily accessible context in which the individual can demonstrate high confidence in science as represented by Western medicine. Here is an institution which, in a certain sense, represents many of the scientific, rational values of the society. It is probably one of the few accessible institutional contexts in which the individual immigrant can openly demonstrate his strong adherence to such values.

In sum, the immigrant populations under study may be said to be characterized by a number of needs. Different subgroups among them will be characterized by higher or lower levels of these needs. The needs have been described as: the need for catharsis; the need to cope with failure; the need to be integrated into Israeli society; the need to attain status; and the need to resolve a magic-science conflict.

Each of the needs is related to a specific latent function of the medical institution. Our analysis proposes that people characterized by a high level of any of these needs will be particularly likely to seek satisfaction for it within the medical context. Such people may be thought of as "utilizing" the institution for its latent as well as for its manifest functions. The availability and convenient accessibility of Kupat Holim make it a particularly attractive locus to satisfy such needs.

ADOPTING THE SICK ROLE

Nevertheless, we cannot propose that all people with a need will seek satisfaction for it through Kupat Holim, even if they are aware of its potential in this direction. Other contexts to satisfy needs may be available to them. Merton (1949) has made the point that people will seek to satisfy needs through the latent functions of an institution when alternatives are blocked or less available. We have already noted that there may be a certain press toward utilizing the Kupat Holim alternative particularly because of its relatively easy accessibility. However, this does not eliminate the possibility of alternative sources of need satisfaction. It is even possible that such satisfaction could be obtained in another medical context, that is, from a private practitioner or other clinic facilities. For example, one could easily envision the possibility of the individual satisfying his need for catharsis elsewhere, with a social worker, rabbi, or indeed, within a family or neighborly context. With respect to a magic-science conflict, there might also be other contexts in which a high level of confidence in science could be expressed. Other of the needs, most markedly the need for coping with failure, push strongly toward the necessity of obtaining satisfaction from the Kupat Holim clinic: in effect, there are practically no alternatives to this, except, perhaps, the private practitioner. In any case, the analysis requires that we define the conditions under which the Kupat Holim alternative is likely to be the one chosen to satisfy the need.

In an attempt to filter out those people who would be likely to turn to Kupat Holim to obtain satisfaction of their needs, we have made use of a variable used by Mechanic and Volkart (1960; Mechanic, 1962), the "tendency to adopt the sick role." We have adopted their position that this tendency can be defined in terms of a continuum. This is to say that there is no absolute point at which all individuals enter the sick role. The adoption of the sick role is a subjective matter and can be thought of as a function of a wide variety of needs and predispositions. In the case of our study, it is undoubtedly also a function of different cultural definitions.

Given a number of ambiguous symptoms of the sort that could be interpreted either as serious or insignificant, some individuals will interpret such symptoms in order to move themselves into the sick role. Others will either ignore the symptoms or interpret them in such a way as not to define themselves as sick. The point to be emphasized is that varying tendencies will appear among different individuals or groups having the same objective symptoms (Kasl and Cobb, 1966).

We are suggesting that the tendency to adopt the sick role may help filter out those individuals who are likely to turn to the Kupat Holim alternative to obtain satisfaction of a need. Such a tendency implies a comparatively greater readiness to turn to Kupat Holim. In a sense, Kupat Holim is more salient to these people than it is to others, and they will presumably be oriented more than others toward the Kupat Holim institutional context.

Our hypotheses are therefore formulated, not in terms of the need alone and the latent function, but in terms of the need *combined with* the tendency to adopt the sick role as motivating the individual to seek out the latent function of the institution. The paradigm for the hypotheses involves five different needs but the "tendency to adopt the sick role" is used systematically with respect to each. We therefore have five predictions, each stating that individuals with a high level of need *and* a tendency to adopt the sick role will be most likely to seek out the latent function of the institution corresponding to that need.

Empirically we have chosen to dichotomize each of the need variables as well as the tendency variable. The result for each of the needs is a fourfold typology in which the prediction applies to one type only. Of course, we are unable to say that people falling in any of the other three types will fail completely to take advantage of the latent functions of the institutions; what we predict is that the group with the high need *and* the tendency to adopt the sick role (referred to in the text from now on as the critical group), will be more likely than the remaining groups to utilize the latent functions of the institution.

The paradigm may be somewhat clearer if we reintroduce examples from the substantive needs and latent functions already discussed. It will be recalled that we referred to needs for catharsis, coping with failure, integration, status, and resolution of a magic-science conflict—as well as the latent functions of the institution complementing each of these. Substantively, the hypothesis proposes that people with a high need for catharsis *and* with a tendency to adopt the sick role will attempt to satisfy this need through the institution. The same prediction is made for each of the other needs.

It does not follow that any one individual or any one group of individuals will necessarily be motivated by *all* of these needs simultaneously, or correspondingly, will seek out all of the latent functions. At the same time, there could be motivation from more than one need and an attempt to gain satisfaction from more than one latent function. This may be where the pattern of high level utilization ties in.

We have referred to the dependent variables as the process of "utilizing," "taking advantage of," or "gaining satisfaction from" the institution. This proved to be a tricky variable to define, particularly in an interview situation. The hypotheses require, however, that a measure for the satisfaction of each need be formulated.

The approach taken focuses on the client's point of view in terms of his patterns of perception of the institution. Since the client is the principal recipient of the institution's services, it would seem appropriate to base ourselves on *his* judgments and opinions concerning the institution in our efforts to analyze its latent functions. While other points of view play a role—for example, that of the physician or of other official Kupat Holim personnel—they represent *intentions* rather than actual delivery: Kupat Holim physicians may believe they provide patients with an opportunity to speak freely of their problems thus satisfying a need for catharsis. But patients may perceive the same situation quite differently and could find such behavior inadequate in terms of their own felt needs. It is therefore essential to focus the analysis on clients' perception patterns in an attempt to analyze the structure of the latent functions of the institution. Accordingly, five perception variables were formulated to complement each of the latent functions.

We assume that members of the "critical group" are characterized by heightened expectations of the institution with respect to each latent function. This is because a high level of need sets up a certain pressure to obtain satisfaction for it and increases the likelihood that appropriate situations will be recognized as potentially fulfilling the need. This means, for example, that people with a need for catharsis will feel pressure to satisfy this need and will be more likely than others to perceive Kupat Holim as a possible context to satisfy it. The same would be true of people with a high need for coping with failure, integration into Israeli society, status, and resolution of a magic-science conflict.

The reality of Kupat Holim is such, however, that expectations of this sort are not always met. There are many deviations from the ideal patterns which generate the latent functions we have described: physicians do not always behave in the expected manner nor do patients always carry out the patient role appropriately. The interaction between the two can sometimes result in situations which are markedly different from the ideal patterns we have described earlier. Some of the sources for these deviations will be spelled out in the following section on physicians' response patterns to patients' needs.

Even if the critical group is characterized by higher expectations than others with respect to the latent functions of the institution, it is evident that it may succeed *or* fail in realizing them, depending on the nature of the experience in Kupat Holim. High expectations lead us to predict a polarity in the perception of the institution by the critical group: it will be higher than the other three groups in perceiving the institution as satisfying the need when the latent function is successfully activated; it will be lower than the other three groups when the latent function fails to be activated. Such polarity is a result of relatively high expectations which, we hypothesize, will cause the critical group to respond to the institution in more extreme terms.

The more specific formulation of the hypotheses with respect to the five latent functions focuses on this polarity of the dependent variable. Stated in its testable form, each of the five hypotheses proposes that individuals with a high level of need and a tendency to adopt the sick role will be either significantly higher or significantly lower than the other three groups in perceiving the medical institution as satisfying that need by means of the latent function.

The empirical definitions of the variables utilized to test each of the five hypotheses are spelled out in the chapters dealing with each of the latent functions.

LATENT FUNCTIONS AND CLINIC UTILIZATION

Making use of the basic typology defined by need and the tendency to adopt the sick role, we have asked whether high utilization rates could be associated with apparent success or failure to enjoy the latent functions of the medical institution. Is there evidence that people in the critical group who succeed in utilizing the institution for its latent functions are especially frequent clinic users? Such a pattern would suggest that the latent function is, at least partially, motivating attendance. Are those members of the critical group who perceive the institution as not providing for the latent functions particularly high utilizers? If so, this would suggest a possible ritualistic pattern in which clients expect satisfaction of a need through one of the latent functions and continue coming to the clinic for this purpose despite repeated frustration. In such a situation expectations would seem to be overriding reality.

In order to gain insight into these questions the critical group was divided into those who ostensibly satisfy the need and those who do not, and frequency of clinic utilization compared among these groups and the other three. Such an analysis permits us to draw some conclusions about the possible relationship between high utilization rates and the latent functions of the medical institution.

The overall framework of our analysis has been formulated in terms of role complementarity. There are two sides to the relationship with which we are dealing: the *patient,* who has been viewed in terms of his needs and his perception of the institution as a potential locus to satisfy them, and the *physician,* who is considered in terms of his response to the patient and to the patient's needs. Role complementarity requires a certain congruence between the two parties to the relationship (Henderson, 1935; Szasz and Hollender, 1956).

In discussing the relationship of the physician's role to the latent function of the medical institution, we have referred to the ideal pattern that should structure the physician's professional relationship to his patients. Reasonable conformity to this pattern would seem to be necessary for the latent functions of the medical institution to appear. On an ideal level the Western medical profession requires that doctors' orientation toward patients be universalistic, specific, nonaffective, and collectivity-oriented (Parsons, 1951). From this point of view, only the patient's illness is relevant to the relationship; other characteristics, such as ethnic origin, family background, work history, are relevant only insofar as they contribute to diagnosis or treatment. Affect-laden norms are not admitted as relevant in the professional relationship. The physician perceives the patient qua patient and nothing more. The patient and the physician should, from this point of view, be oriented to jointly agreed upon therapeutic or curative goals.

This ideal pattern may, however, be either modified or changed as a result of various pressures and norms impinging on the physician. These will affect his role performance and in some cases prevent the latent functions from appearing. In such situations patients' needs and expectations may not be fully met by the medical institution.

The factors that modify the ideal pattern of the physician's relationship to his patient stem from four major sources: behavior of patients, norms of the society, situational factors, and group memberships.

One condition that seems essential for the physician to behave in accordance with the ideal professional model is the general conformity of the patient to norms of Western patient behavior. These include acceptance of the physician's authority, attitudes of respect, following instructions, personal and environmental cleanliness, and sanitation. Furthermore, the physician may expect the patient to bring him an essentially *medical* problem, defined within reasonable margins. The breadth of these margins will, of course, differ among physicians, depending on their own definition of medical problems. It is also worth noting that home remedies and the use of traditional medical practices and practitioners are not considered legitimate for a Western patient. The doctor may also expect the patient to want to get better and to cooperate in reaching that goal.

To the extent that a patient deviates from any of these norms it may be assumed that the physician's perception of him will shift. Rather than perceiving him as a patient, the physician will categorize him as a nonconforming patient. This shift in the category of perception will be reflected in the doctor's pattern of orientation in particular in an increase in affectivity. His collectivity orientation, which dictates that both he and the patient are striving toward a common goal, that is, the patient's health, may also shift toward the goal of getting the patient to adopt more Western patient norms. This may not be at all what the patient wants.

Certain types of patients may impress the physician as simulating illness or as attending his clinic with unnecessary frequency. He may be convinced, rightly or wrongly, that these patients are attempting to gain other rewards through claims of illness. In such cases, the category of perception will be shifted from "patient" to "malingerer" or "hypochondriac." Not only do these categorizations remove the client from the physician's legitimate area of activity, but they may arouse considerable affect in him, mostly because such clients press him to deviate from his professional therapeutic role (Field, 1957).

One ideal norm of Israeli society is a strong equalitarianism. The historical bases for this norm can be traced to socialist Zionist ideology, democratic political orientations, and the value of *kibbutz galuyot* (ingathering of the exiles) toward which the society is strongly oriented and which prescribes equality for groups of all ethnic origins. Furthermore the specific institutional context of Kupat Holim within which the physician works has, like any medical organization, norms of its own, prescribing behavior with respect to patients. Medical norms of Kupat Holim stem from its historic association with the Histadrut and with the overall goals of the society, both of which push strongly toward equalitarianism.

At the same time, there is some evidence that this ideal norm coexists with certain contradictory attitudes and behavior patterns. Israeli observers have noted the development of patterns of differential orientation and prejudice focused particularly on people from Near Eastern and North African countries. While this prejudice is not institutionalized and certainly does not take the extreme form found in some other countries, it does express itself in selective social relationships and stereotyping (Shuval, 1956; 1962a).

Clearly these two attitudes of equalitarianism and prejudice conflict. Since the latter is fairly widespread in Israeli society, physicians, who are overwhelmingly European, may well have internalized some of it. It would probably be difficult for a physician to be so committed to a universalistic norm that he could be impervious to these attitudes. To the extent that he has internalized some of them, categorization of clients may occur in terms of ethnic modifiers with accompanying stereotypes and negative affect. While the full detailed range of ethnic identification may not be utilized, certain gross ethnic dimensions, because of their high visibility, probably will. Thus, it may not be possible for the physician to identify a patient in terms of his specific country of origin but it will be almost inevitable that he be categorized as a European or non-European. Furthermore, specific ethnic groups may stand out in the physician's field of perception: his own, or groups toward which there are fairly clearly structured attitudes in the society, for example, Moroccans and Yemenites. This orientation violates the ideal norm of universalism and introduces a variety of other categories of perception with accompanying modification of the ideal pattern of orientation.

The individual physician will behave in terms of his own personal mode of internalizing general medical norms. Thus he personally may accept or reject certain of the norms of the profession. Furthermore, he may personally accept or reject Kupat Holim norms. His own definition of his professional role may prescribe that he focus on the medical problem in its narrowest sense, or that he view the patient in his broadest context with the latter's social characteristics as highly relevant to his illness. Furthermore, the physician may view himself as a teacher. The societal norms will also be internalized by each physician in an individual manner and will express themselves accordingly.

The bureaucratically organized clinic reinforces some aspects of the physician's ideal pattern of orientation. In its classic form, the bureaucratic structure reinforces universalism, specificity, and nonaffectivity in the bureaucrat's relationship to his client. The presence of colleagues and the more public nature of his professional performance pressure the physician working within a bureaucratic medical structure to adhere more stringently to ideal medical norms. He has less freedom to deviate since he is under more constant scrutiny than the solo practitioner (Freidson, 1960). It is further worth noting that the technical medical facilities available within a medical bureaucratic organization facilitate professional role performance by the individual physician.

At the same time the bureaucratically organized clinic puts certain pressures on the physician, often forcing him to modify his professional role. As in most bureaucracies, the Kupat Holim physician finds himself inundated with paper work of various sorts. Some of this is related to organizational aspects of the bureaucracy while some concerns medical records or other documents needed by patients. Since few of the clinics employ adequate secretarial help and many do not have a nurse to deal with these matters, the burden often falls heavily on the physician himself. Of the physicians in our study, 79 per cent reported that they were disturbed by excessive paper work.

This feeling of disturbance affects professional role performance in at least two ways. One is the feeling of time wasted at the expense of professional treatment and care of patients. The other is the feeling of being a clerk, which, with the considerably lower status suggested by this occupation, undermines the self-image of the Kupat Holim physician.

The freedom inherent in the professional role is distorted by the Kupat Holim bureaucracy through a multitude of instructions to personnel issued from those in authority and particularly by the requirement to accept a given number of patients per hour. The latter is especially offensive since it undermines much of the freedom and flexibility required by physicians in carrying out their professional obligations (Ben David, 1958).

These pressures may result in inadequate time allotment to patients and possibly in a generalized dissatisfaction, both of which cause the doctor to deviate from his ideal nonaffectively oriented role. A build-up of such pressures could, in the context of prejudice referred to above, result in focusing hostility on specific ethnic groups.

A physician's behavior is further affected by his own group memberships. Only 5 per cent of the doctors in our population were born in a non-European country. Furthermore, 16 per cent were of Rumanian origin, a factor of some relevance to the Rumanian patient population with which we are dealing. Communication will probably be structured differently between a physician and a patient from his own specific country of origin (Lieberson, 1958). The same is true for his class membership which will determine the status gap between himself and his client. This means that salient group memberships may divert the physician from the ideal universalistic pattern of orientation to clients.

The total effect of these several factors on the physician's role performance could shift the ideal pattern of orientation in a number of directions. We have seen that certain pressures push the doctor away from a strictly universalistic orientation in the direction of greater particularism. There is also pressure toward affectivity and toward increased self-orientation with a probable loss of emphasis on collectivity orientation. The five needs of patients are differentially satisfied by various elements comprising the physician's ideal pattern of orientation. It is important to consider the impact of these possible changes of the physician's pattern of orientation to clients.

Increased particularism on the part of the physician means that the patient is related to less qua patient and more in terms of categories which are not strictly relevant to the medical context. In our case the most prominent of these are ethnic and class modifiers of the patient category. The awareness that he is treating a person of a given ethnic or class origin will condition the physician's willingness or ability to satisfy that patient's needs. When the cultural or status gap between physician and patient is great, the doctor may respond less to certain of the patient's needs; when the gap is small, the likelihood of a positive response to certain types of needs would seem to be greater. In other words, a particularistic orientation, by bringing medically irrelevant categories into play, results in differential response patterns by physicians to different types of patients.

The shift from a nonaffective to an affective pattern of orientation would probably result in a generalized lowered willingness to respond favorably to the needs of patients. (We are referring here to negative affect.) When the doctor is frustrated and annoyed, he will tend to be less tolerant of patients' needs. Although such hostility may be directed primarily toward those patients who seem to be the source of the frustration, for example, those who conform least to Western patient norms, the aggression may be generalized and displaced to other patients as well.

The shift from an emphasis on collectivity orientation to a greater emphasis on self-orientation results in a heightened concern by the physician with his own professional role performance and image. Such self-orientation may result in a somewhat lowered sensitivity to patients' needs—particularly the latent ones—and less willingness to satisfy them.

In considering physicians' response to patients, we focus specifically on the relevance of patients' ethnic affiliation. In particular we compare physicians' orientations to a European and to a non-European group.

It would seem that two quite different patterns of response could occur. On the whole European patients are characterized by greater conformity to Western patient norms as well as by more education and greater sophistication than non-Europeans. These qualities would be likely to make it easier for physicians to adhere to an ideal pattern of professional orientation in their relations with Europeans. This would imply more negative affect in relations with patients from North African and Near Eastern countries and less of a collectivity orientation. Such negative affect makes it less likely that physicians will respond or be sensitive to the needs of such patients. If they are perceived as a source of professional frustration, physicians will be more prone to find direct or indirect ways of expressing hostility toward them.

On the other hand, a wide culture gap between physician and patient could result in lowered expectations on the part of physicians: patients who are "ignorant," "primitive," or "uncultured" cannot really be expected to conform to Western standards of behavior. From this point of view it is somehow more acceptable for non-Europeans than for Europeans to display nonconforming patterns of patient behavior. Thus physicians would be more tolerant of deviance by non-Europeans and more demanding in their expectations that Europeans live up to the standards of Western patient behavior.

In sum, we expect physicians' orientation to non-European patients to be characterized by relatively more hostility, less willingness to respond to needs, but comparatively high tolerance to deviance from the ideal patient role. With respect to European patients, physicians would be likely to reveal comparatively less hostility, greater willingness to respond to needs, but more stringent demands for conformity to the ideal patient role.

2

Method and Field Procedures

The theoretical problems posed required the collection of two sets of data: one from Kupat Holim members and another from Kupat Holim physicians. Ideally it might have been desirable to match the needs and perceptions of the individual member with the behavior of his individual physician, but practically, it was not feasible. The two sets of data were therefore collected separately.

Our interest in Kupat Holim members as a whole precluded the possibility of using clinic attenders as our subjects. The self-selection of the latter population made it inappropriate for testing the proposed hypotheses. The central concern with high clinic utilization and its correlates made it essential that infrequent utilizers and nonutilizers also be included among the subjects of study. This meant that Kupat Holim membership and not clinic attendance was the primary criterion for inclusion in the study population.

31

Interest in the acculturation process required a focus on a population of immigrants. Immigrants were defined as persons who arrived in Israel after the establishment of the state in 1948. Four specific groups were chosen: Jews from Kurdistan, Morocco, Rumania, and Poland. These groups differ from each other on two major dimensions which are relevant to the theoretical problems under study: (1) degree of traditionalism with respect to social relations and values, and (2) extent of experience with Western medicine, especially of the bureaucratic variety that characterizes Kupat Holim. The Kurds are the most traditional of these groups and have had the least experience with Western medicine; the Rumanians and Poles are the least traditional and have had the most experience with Western medicine. The Moroccans fall between. Chapter Three, The Ethnic Groups, provides descriptive material on these ethnic groups. We have not included nonimmigrants for comparison but have focused on comparisons among and within these groups.

In an attempt to learn about the differential effects of the clinic setting, a rural and an urban group of immigrant members of Kupat Holim was included from each ethnic group. The only exception were the Poles who, for technical reasons, were selected only from urban residents. This design yielded seven "ethnic-residential" groups and called for interviewing about 300 men and women over the age of twenty in each.

Sampling of ethnic groups represents a thorny problem in Israel. Complete lists of residents by country of origin are not available. Kupat Holim records, both in the local clinics and in the national files, were uneven and often incomplete with respect to accurate information on members' country of origin.

Since this study does not aim to generalize its findings to the ethnic groups as a whole, the sampling problem is not crucial. It is sufficient to include groups of immigrants from the required countries of origin, in adequate numbers to permit statistical analysis, and without gross or obvious biases in their demographic characteristics.

The approach followed was to seek concentrations of the desired ethnic groups in urban and in rural settings and to include all persons in those locations meeting the following criteria: (1)

Kupat Holim membership, (2) Kurdish, Moroccan, Rumanian, or Polish origin, and (3) arrival in Israel after May 1948. Among those who met the criteria, men and women over twenty were interviewed alternately on the basis of instructions given in advance by the fieldwork supervisor. Since there was no known policy of selective settlement of immigrants in these areas, it was felt that the policy of interviewing all persons with the required characteristics in the area would prevent gross biases. A total of 1,907 Kupat Holim members were interviewed during the spring and summer of 1962, of whom 1,076 lived in cities and 831 in rural settings.

The urban subjects were located by focusing on immigrant quarters of Jerusalem, Beersheba, and Holon, in which heavy concentrations of the relevant ethnic groups lived. Examination of the Kupat Holim records in these neighborhoods found them to be incomplete with respect to information on members' country of origin. In some clinics we were able to obtain the assistance of the clerk, who was personally acquainted with all members, to filter out the ineligibles. In other cases the entire membership list served as the gross list of eligibles and inappropriate subjects were eliminated after a home visit revealed that they did not fit our criteria. Of 1,323 eligible subjects located in this manner, 1,076 were successfully interviewed: 81 per cent of the potential. The remainder were not found at home after three visits or refused to be interviewed. The urban group therefore consists of 311 Moroccans, 258 Kurds, 270 Rumanians, and 237 Poles.

The rural populations were drawn from *moshavim* (cooperative villages). These are small agricultural villages usually composed of less than 100 families. This type of settlement was chosen because it is the principal form of rural settlement for immigrants used in the past twenty years (Israel Central Bureau of Statistics, 1963). *Moshavim* were selected in which there was known to be a high concentration of immigrants from the relevant countries. Interviewing took place in eleven *moshavim* with concentrations of Moroccan immigrants, seven with concentrations of Kurds, and nine with concentrations of Rumanians. A Kupat Holim clinic exists in all of these communities and all residents are members. Teams of interviewers made up of two to five persons worked together in an attempt to complete interviewing in any one *moshav* as rapidly as

possible. Of the 1,156 subjects in the *moshavim,* 831 were successfully interviewed: 72 per cent of the potential. The remainder were
not found after three visits, were found to be ineligible through the
inaccurate recording of background data, or refused. The rural
group, therefore, consists of 286 Moroccans, 264 Kurds, and 281
Rumanians.

While there was no attempt to sample the ethnic residential
groups or to generalize to the wider populations from which they
are drawn, it is nevertheless of some interest to compare our study
populations, insofar as this is possible, with data reported in the 1961
Census. The Census reports the distribution of immigrants by country of origin, date of immigration, and age (Israel Central Bureau
of Statistics, 1963). Such a comparison shows that the urban
Moroccans in our study, most of whom immigrated to Israel between 1948 and 1951, are almost identical in their age structure
to the population from which they were drawn. The other groups
are somewhat younger but the differences are not large. In general
it is easier to interview younger subjects and the refusal rate is
usually higher among older people. Furthermore, the decision to
interview the head of the household or his wife alternately undoubtedly eliminated some older segments of the population: when
older parents or grandparents were living with a family they were
not included while the younger head of household or his wife was.
Since we were not interested in including people who are especially
likely to be physically ill or particularly sensitive to health problems,
such a bias in favor of a younger population is to the advantage of
our design. The Census does not provide additional breakdowns
for comparison.

For the physician population the study design directed us to
focus on general practitioners rather than on specialists. Visiting a
specialist compels a greater focus on the narrow medical aspects of
the problem, while visiting the general practitioner, with his broader
range of concern, is a less narrowly defined situation in which nonmedical needs of patients can find expression more readily, since a
general practitioner can be legitimately visited with fairly vague
medical symptoms. This permits freer play for nonmedical needs
of patients. Different types of specialists also vary in the nature of
their practices and it would have been difficult to question Kupat

Holim members about any one type; such variation would have greatly complicated the analysis. It was therefore decided to limit the population of physicians to one type only: the type most likely to activate the latent functions. While our theoretical analysis applies to some extent to specialists, it is focused on general practitioners and they were therefore chosen as the population to be studied.

It was intended to include physicians in both rural and urban practices—to parallel the rural and urban populations of Kupat Holim members. This would have made possible a comparative analysis of problems of practice in these two settings. Unfortunately, the number of doctors from rural clinics participating in the study was too small to permit separate analysis.

Data concerning physicians were obtained during the spring and summer of 1962 in the course of a series of seventeen meetings in all fifteen administrative districts of Kupat Holim. Invitations explaining the nature of the research and signed by the district medical officer in each district were sent to all general practitioners in the area. Fifteen to forty doctors attended each of these meetings, which was also attended and directed by two members of the research team. At these meetings participants completed a questionnaire and participated in an open, unstructured discussion concerning high clinic utilization in Israel and problems of practice in a heterogeneous immigrant society. This was tape-recorded and is used as qualitative and illustrative material in the analysis.

Of the 1,162 general practitioners working in the district clinics of Kupat Holim, 342 (29 per cent) attended these meetings. Since attendance was voluntary, the group that attended is self-selected and cannot be considered a sample of the population. However, comparison of the physicians participating in the study with the total population of general practitioners in Kupat Holim shows few differences in terms of their age, sex, or countries of origin (Kupat Holim, 1962). It is therefore our impression that interest, curiosity, and possible acceptance of the district medical officer's authority were the major factors motivating attendance and participation.

Two questionnaires were used, one for members of Kupat Holim and one for the physicians. Both were made up largely of closed questions. For many of the variables Guttman scales were defined; otherwise typologies were constructed. In some cases individual items were used in the analysis.

The questionnaire for Kupat Holim members included questions in the following major areas: background data, feelings of health or sickness, the five needs (for catharsis, coping with failure, integration, status, and traditional orientation), the five perception variables paralleling each of the needs, the tendency to define oneself as ill, data on frequency of clinic attendance, and attitudes toward and satisfaction with Kupat Holim.

Two pretests were run of this questionnaire. Both took place in the spring and summer of 1961 in Jerusalem in areas in which it was decided not to carry out the final interviewing. Since the questionnaire for rural Kupat Holim members was identical, no pretest was done in rural areas. The first pretest covered seventy-three members of the four ethnic groups. Subjects meeting the criteria of Kupat Holim membership, arrival in Israel after 1948, and membership in one of the ethnic groups were chosen by the interviewers in a number of Jerusalem neighborhoods. Considerable editing took place after the first pretest.

The second pretest covered seventy-seven subjects. The procedure was much the same as in the first pretest. With minor changes the questionnaire was found ready to take into the field.

Experience in the field showed there to be substantial numbers of Polish and Rumanian subjects who did not know Hebrew well enough to be freely interviewed in that language. The questionnaire was accordingly translated into Yiddish, Polish, and Rumanian and the written version was used by interviewers knowing these languages when necessary. Most of the Kurdish and Moroccan subjects knew sufficient Hebrew to be freely interviewed. For the few who did not, the questionnaire was translated orally by an interviewer knowing French, Moroccan, Arabic, or Kurdish. Interviews were conducted in the homes of respondents and averaged slightly over an hour.

The physician questionnaire was designed to determine doctors' response to patients' needs. It included questions in the following major areas: background data, filter questions determining whether the physician had treated fifty or more patients from each of the ethnic groups during the past year, response to the five needs of patients, beliefs of the physician as to how he should behave under ideal circumstances, doctors' perception of colleagual and institutional norms concerning response to patients' needs.

It was impossible to run a pretest of the physicians' questionnaire because the entire population of general practitioners was viewed as potential subjects. The text was therefore checked carefully by a number of individual doctors and editing done on the basis of their comments.

One major focus of the theoretical analysis concerns response of physicians to different ethnic groups of patients. This parallels the analysis of expectations expressed by different ethnic groups of Kupat Holim members with respect to the physician. In order to keep responses as reality-bound as possible, only those physicians with experience in treating at least fifty patients from the specific ethnic group during the past year were asked to report on their attitudes toward patients of this group. An insufficient number of doctors reported experience with Kurdish patients; the analysis is therefore limited to physicians' reports of the attitudes toward Moroccan and Rumanian patients. There are no differences in age, sex, year of immigration to Israel, and length of time in practice between physicians reporting attitudes toward Moroccan patients and those reporting attitudes toward Rumanian patients. There were also ninety-two doctors who reported having fifty Moroccan as well as fifty Rumanian patients during the past year, but when they are analyzed separately the findings are no different.

It is of some importance to bear in mind that response to patients' need is measured by physicians' reports of their behavior in an anonymous written questionnaire completed in a group setting. When topics are raised which threaten professional, social, or personal norms, the possibility must be considered of some distortion of physicians' reports—probably in the direction of conformity to such norms. However, when the data show differences among groups of physicians, *despite* the existence of these norms, we have all the more reason to believe that such differences—or even more pronounced differences—exist on a behavioral level.

3

Ethnic Groups

To get a clear picture of the four immigrant groups included in this study, we present a brief ethnographic sketch of each of them—not a complete descriptive picture, but a general summary of the cultural patterns that characterized these groups before their immigration to Israel. (For a more complete picture, the reader is referred to the ethnographic bibliography at the end of the book.) The groups were chosen, among other reasons, because of the different levels of traditionalism that characterize them. It was assumed that such traditionalism was more or less inversely related to contact with Western-style medical practice: the most traditional groups had least such contact and experience before immigration to Israel while the least traditional groups had the most. Although the available source material provides only sketchy information concerning specific prior experience with Western-style medicine, it is possible to learn a good deal about the extent of traditionalism and Westernization that characterized the groups.

We have attempted to cull from the literature whatever

information was available concerning attitudes and practices relating to health and medicine. In several cases the information
available refers to such topics as childbirth practices or prenatal and
postnatal care. We have generally included this type of material
because of the light it can shed on the group's overall orientation
to health problems and their correlates.

The period described covers approximately the years since
the turn of the century with a particular focus on the post-World-
War-I years. This represents a total period of roughly fifty years
before the populations studied immigrated to Israel. Persons who
arrived in Israel as adults grew up in the social and cultural contexts of their native countries during this period. We have tried to
point up features of these Jewish communities which were more or
less typical of their social and cultural life, taking into account the
considerable social and political change that characterized this
period.

The literature on which this limited ethnographic survey is
based is uneven in terms of its reliability and completeness. Some
sources represent impressionistic statements; others are based on
more serious ethnographic research. Since we view this material only
as supportive and as background information to the main substance
of this book, we have simply taken the sources for what they are
worth and summarized the major observations recorded.

KURDISH IMMIGRANTS

While Kurdish tribes live in portions of Iran, Iraq, Syria,
Turkey, and the USSR (Armenia), the Jewish communities were
located principally in the Mosul area in the northeastern part of
Iraq, with smaller numbers in Iran and Turkey. The Jews lived
in isolated villages in the comparatively inaccessible mountainous
regions of these countries under social and economic conditions
that had not changed very much for hundreds of years. Life in these
villages was comparatively unaffected by social and political changes
in other parts of the world so that many traditional cultural patterns
continued to flourish unchanged. In terms of their basic traditionalism, Kurdish Jews bore a remarkable similarity to their non-Jewish
neighbors, although the substance of their social and cultural life
was different.

The fact that they lived in several different countries makes it difficult to determine the size of the Kurdish Jewish community. The most reasonable estimate appears to be about 50,000 around the time of the establishment of the state of Israel but it is unclear how they were distributed among the various political entities (Feitelson, 1954). Almost all of the Kurdish Jews in Iraq, where the largest community lived, immigrated to Israel. Somewhat smaller proportions came from the other countries. It is also difficult to estimate the number of Kurdish Jews in Israel, again because of the diversity of their countries of origin. The census records country of birth but does not indicate ethnic origin, such as Kurdish.

Kurdish Jews lived in small towns in which they formed subcommunities with institutions of their own. Their most common occupations were dyeing and weaving. However they were also peddlers, porters, gold- and silversmiths, and farmers. It is of considerable interest that even when they engaged primarily in non-agricultural occupations, they always did some farming or growing of livestock on the side. In almost all cases their occupations involved physical labor.

Family organization among the Jews was similar in many respects to that of the non-Jewish Kurds. The pattern was one of an extended family system organized along patrilineal, patrilocal lines. Each nuclear family of the household had a room to itself. Family units were never very large because of low life expectancy; estimates are that an average of two sons reached the age of marriage and succeeded in establishing families. This household was both an economic and a political unit.

The preferred marriage pattern was to the daughter of the paternal uncle, and was arranged by the parents to take place at an early age, that is, at seventeen or eighteen for boys and twelve or thirteen for girls. Bride price was paid. Sex role differentiation was marked, with the male spending most of his time with his father and brothers while the wife was with her mother-in-law and the other women in the household. Women were occupied entirely with pregnancies, child care, and household tasks. Authority rested completely with the male head of the household who guarded this position and its honor jealously.

The position of the woman became more important with increased age and especially when she took charge of her own daughters-in-law. Prior to this her role was subordinate and generally submissive. On the whole it can be said that sex roles were structured along traditional lines and were little influenced by processes of modernization.

Boys were preferred to girls. They were sent to receive a traditional religious education when they reached the age of four to six. Few continued beyond the age of thirteen and many left well before then. Poor instruction and lack of support for continued education by family or community members resulted in a generally low level of education among the Kurdish Jews. Girls received no formal education but were trained by the mother for traditional female tasks.

Although the smaller, more isolated villages did not always have a synagogue of their own, the Kurdish Jews adhered closely to traditional religious practices of *kashrut,* Sabbath observance, and family purity. The Bible was widely known by the men but little of the other traditional literature was studied. When the village did not have its own religious functionary, a traveling *chacham* would come at intervals to provide information and perform the necessary religious rituals. The festivals were regularly and elaborately observed.

Magic and superstition played a major role in the life of the Kurdish Jews and were thought of as part and parcel of their religious practice. Talismans and charms were in regular use, particularly as a means of protection against spirits and the evil eye. Dreams were taken to have important meaning and their interpretation was undertaken by a special expert, the chacham. Jews, as well as their non-Jewish neighbors, believed that they could prevent illness and misfortune by means of secret writings and other rituals. The Kurdish Jews also believed in the usefulness of pilgrimages to the graves of well-known persons or prophets where miracles and cures were reputed to occur.

These beliefs formed part of a more general fatalistic orientation which held that events in an individual's life are determined by forces over which he has little control. There is little free choice according to this orientation and one's fate is determined by powers beyond one's control.

It was thought that illness was caused by magic in the form of the evil eye or spirits. Treatment was therefore viewed in terms of counter-magic, that is, talismans, magical prohibitions, or specific rituals. Mental deficiency was also considered a form of disease and cures were attempted by prescribed rituals. It was thought to be useful, for example, to put almonds under the head of such a child at night and have him eat them in the morning.

Pregnancy, birth, and child care were also surrounded by many magical beliefs and rituals. These were aimed to protect the welfare of the child and particularly to prevent possible effects of the evil eye. Since male babies were preferred, the pregnant woman was carefully watched for signs that indicate the sex of the new baby; for example, if the pregnant woman showed a liking for lemon, this was taken as a sign that the baby would be a girl.

Little information is available in the literature concerning the Kurdish Jews' experience with medical institutions and health services. What does emerge clearly is the traditional quality of their social life and their isolation from most Western influences.

MOROCCAN IMMIGRANTS

The Moroccans were included in the study because of their transitional status between a traditional society and a modern, Western-oriented social system.

Before the French Protectorate, which was established in Morocco in 1912, the Jewish population lived, as it had for many centuries, as a small minority within a Moslem majority. During this long period the Jews were strongly influenced by the surrounding Moslem community and its traditional cultural patterns. On the whole little change took place in the society until the arrival of the French.

As nonbelievers, the Jews were defined by the Moslems as *dhimmi*—protegés of the sultan—and as such occupied a separate status which entailed numerous disabilities: they were required to wear special black clothing, remove their shoes in the vicinity of a mosque, forbidden to ride horses, carry arms, marry Moslems, or build houses higher than Moslems. A long history of persecution by the Moslems was combined with a sort of tolerance of the Jews as clearly defined second-class citizens.

During several hundred years preceding the establishment of the French Protectorate the Jews lived in enclosed areas of the Moslem towns, the *mellah*. Here they carried on a well developed religious and community life. A council of elders handled all matters relating to births, deaths, charity, education, synagogues, ritual baths, slaughterhouses, and religious courts. There was a representative of the Jewish community to the sultan whose task included collection of taxes, and recruitment of manpower, but community life functioned on an almost completely independent basis inside the *mellah*.

The Jews were occupied mostly as artisans and concentrated principally in jewelry making and tailoring. In addition many were small shopkeepers or peddlers.

Family life inside the *mellah* was structured along traditional lines with strong sex-role differentiation. Boys received a traditional *heder* education rarely continuing beyond the age of thirteen when they joined the adult workers. Girls received no formal education but assisted the mother in household tasks and errands from early childhood. Marriage was arranged by the parents at an early age but consummated only at puberty. The role of the wife was seen in traditional terms as childbearer and housekeeper. She was limited strictly to the home and never ventured out unaccompanied. Authority resided with the husband, to whom she owed complete obedience.

The customs and behavior patterns surrounding pregnancy and delivery resembled those of the Moslems and Berbers. The woman was thought to be in a weakened condition during pregnancy and particularly vulnerable to the influence of the evil eye. Rabbis were often invited to the home during this period to try to prevent these evil influences. Delivery took place in the home with the assistance of a traditional midwife, who was an older married woman. Boys were preferred to girls and there were many ritual practices which attempted to insure the birth of a boy.

Disease was traditionally viewed as a sign of God's disfavor.

Spirits and the evil eye were thought of as causative agents and prevention of illness therefore required ritually defined means of pacifying them. This was considered particularly important at times when a person was considered most subject to the influence of these agents, for example, in early infancy or during pregnancy. Planets and stars were also thought to influence the effectiveness of the evil eye. Talismans and secret formulas were viewed as useful preventive mechanisms. People also used to make pilgrimages to caves thought to be inhabited by certain of the spirits. These were believed to be useful in preventing sterility as well.

The establishment of the French Protectorate in 1912 introduced a series of changes in the traditional social structure of Morocco which made themselves felt both in the Moslem and in the Jewish sectors of the population. Although the French abolished many of the formal disabilities to which the Jews were subjected, Moslems did not automatically drop their traditional attitude toward the Jews as *dhimmi*. This ambiguity left the Jews in a more or less ambivalent position—between the newer aspects of the social structure introduced by the French and the traditional Moslem way of life. In some respects the Jews became detached from their traditional way of life, with its security and stability, but they succeeded only partially in adapting themselves to the more modern patterns introduced by the French.

From 1912 on Jews gradually began to move out of the *mellah* and into the newer parts of town. They also started to enter liberal professions and government posts. These trends were especially typical of the more mobile, enterprising and, in most cases, economically well-established Jews. Physical separation from the tightly knit Jewish community of the *mellah* resulted in increased contact and influence from the French and the modern way of life they represented.

A process of growing urbanization began under the French. Many Jews migrated from the villages to the larger towns and from the towns to the major cities. The pattern was for these migrants to move into the *mellahs* and occupy space vacated by Jews who moved out of the *mellahs* into the newer parts of the city.

Health services began to develop during this period. Births took place more frequently in the hospital, but many still took place in the home; women were reluctant to spend more than a minimum of time within the confines of the hospital's unfamiliar environment. From the turn of the century the Alliance Israelite Universelle undertook to improve the very poor sanitary conditions prevailing in the *mellahs*. This organization also introduced a medical program to fight the endemic trachoma and ringworm.

At the turn of the century the Alliance Israelite Universelle also began establishing a network of schools in which the language of instruction and the cultural emphasis were French. Increasing numbers of boys and girls attended these schools until by 1950 an extremely high proportion of the Jewish children were receiving an essentially Western-style education. Over the years of the Protectorate these schools exerted an enormous cumulative influence in effecting a shift away from traditional patterns toward a more modern way of life. For the first time girls were exposed to a modern, secular system of education so that important trends toward modernization appeared with respect to traditional sex roles. In many cases French became the spoken language with Arabic confined more and more to the home. Marriage was delayed and the partners came increasingly to make the decision themselves— usually with parental consent.

The French introduced modern roads, mass media of communication, and the beginnings of industrialization. Those segments of the Jewish community which had moved out of the *mellah* were strongly influenced by these changes and even those segments which remained physically within the *mellah* found their traditional patterns gradually changing. Nevertheless it should be noted that those segments of the Jewish population which did not move out of the *mellah* remained within a compact community structure which generally tended to reinforce the traditional patterns. Most of them remained small shopkeepers, peddlers, and artisans, and many were unskilled laborers. It was this part of the Jewish population that was least subject to the influence of the French.

The latter point is especially relevant to the present volume because it was essentially the more traditional segments of the Jewish community that migrated to Israel during the early 1950s and after Moroccan independence in 1956. The more affluent, better skilled and educated, and more westernized parts of the

Moroccan Jewish population immigrated to France while the group that came to Israel was composed of the poorer, less skilled people. Generally speaking, this group had not yet moved out of the *mellahs* and, while it had already been exposed to certain elements of westernization, it was still characterized by many aspects of the traditional way of life. Even the most modernized of the Moroccan Jewish families continued to maintain traditional patterns in such areas as religious observance, family solidarity, patriarchal authority, and close supervision of young girls.

It is in this sense that we have characterized the Moroccan immigrants in our study as a group in transition: while their background is highly traditional they were influenced by westernizing changes introduced by the French from 1912. The impact of these changes may have been smaller on the group of Moroccan Jews which immigrated to Israel but it was certainly sufficient to begin to undermine many aspects of traditional life.[1]

The extent of these influences is probably structured along axes defined by the immigrant's age and education. Since westernizing influences increased consistently during the forty-odd years between the establishment of the Protectorate and immigration to Israel, we can assume that immigrants who were socialized earlier in this period would be more traditional, while persons who underwent their primary socializing experiences during the later years of the Protectorate would be less traditional in their orientations and more subject to Western influence. Secular education came to be more and more widespread during this period. This means that persons who were over the age of forty-five at the time the present study was carried out experienced their primary socialization before the arrival of the French or during the early years of the French Protectorate, when its influence was only beginning to be felt. The group that was between thirty-five and forty-five years of age at the time of the interview passed its childhood during the middle years of the French Protectorate, when Western influences were making themselves felt increasingly. The youngest group to be interviewed was socialized toward the end of the period of the

---

[1] J. P. Hes (1964) has also referred to the transitional status of the Moroccan immigrants to Israel, placing them between the more traditional Yemenites and the more westernized Poles.

French Protectorate, when Western influences on the Jewish community reached their maximum.

We have already noted the ambivalence that characterized the Moroccan Jewish community in its process of transition from a traditional way of life to a more modern one. The Jews found themselves between the traditionally hostile and increasingly nationalistic Arab community and the French among whom they gained only partial acceptance and whose way of life they succeeded only partially in internalizing. Greater identification with the French generally meant detachment from the security and stability of a traditional way of life. This process had the general effect of placing the most westernized of these Jews in a position of ambivalence between a past which they tended to reject and a new set of values which they had not yet internalized fully. It would seem reasonable to assume that the younger segments of the Moroccan Jewish population would feel this ambivalence most.

In the early 1950s there were an estimated 260,000 Jews in Morocco. The Israel census of 1961 reports that 110,855 immigrated to Israel after the establishment of the state in 1948.

RUMANIAN IMMIGRANTS

After World War I the Kingdom of Rumania, which had been in existence since 1881, more than doubled its territory through the acquisition of Transylvania from Hungary, Bessarabia from Russia, and Bucovina from Austria. These territories included large Jewish populations which differed from each other in their social and historical background. Their annexation to the Old Kingdom brought the total Jewish population of Rumania to three-quarters of a million in 1930.

Before World War I the Jews of the Old Kingdom were largely confined to geographical and social ghettos and deprived of civil rights. During King Carol's reign (1881–1916) many laws were enacted forbidding Jews to live in rural areas, barring them from various trades and professions, and subjecting them to other discriminatory measures. There was considerable emigration of Jews as a result.

During the period preceding World War I the Jews were engaged mainly in commerce, crafts, and small-scale industry. In

Bessarabia, Bucovina, and Transylvania the economic opportunities were somewhat more favorable and Jews were active in the professions as well. They were a highly urbanized group: according to the Rumanian census of 1930, 71.5 per cent of the Jews lived in the towns.

The Jews were organized in communal *kehilot,* which undertook to care for the religious, cultural, social, health, and welfare needs of their members. In almost every community there was a rabbi, ritual-slaughterer, and *melamed* (teacher), as well as a burial society, a charity organization providing aid to the poor and to orphans, and a *bikur cholim,* which provided assistance to the sick. Some of the larger communities also established Jewish hospitals. In some communities there were women's organizations which, among other welfare undertakings, established soup kitchens for the needy and provided medical care and medicines free of charge.

Once united in Rumania, the Jews were subjected to increasingly virulent anti-Semitism. Although the period between 1920 and 1930 was a prosperous one for Rumania, the economic crises of the 1930s and the failure of the new leaders to strengthen and enlarge Rumanian democracy led to a rapid displacement of power from the elected parliament to the crown. Out of these crises rose a Nazi-like organization called the Iron Guard, a fanatically anti-Semitic organization, which openly preached the massacre of the Jews and managed to attain a dominant role in Rumanian life by the mid-thirties. From 1935 on Jews were progressively eliminated from one profession after another, were subjected to continual attacks, both verbal and physical, and over a third were stripped of their citizenship in 1938.

During the twentieth century several new social and cultural trends developed in Rumanian Jewry supplementing the traditional *kehila* structure. Jewish newspapers and books were published in Rumanian, Yiddish, and Hebrew. Hebrew schools (of the *Tarbut* network) as well as Yiddish schools were established and efforts were made by means of lectures, booklets, and summer camps to spread a knowledge of Jewish culture and history. The Zionist movement, with its various political branches, became active and in some parts of Rumania became extremely prominent in Jewish life.

There was also a Jewish political party with the express purpose of representing Jewish interests in parliament. On the whole the Jews of the Old Kingdom tended to be more assimilated while those in Transylvania, Bucovina, and Bessarabia kept up a more active Jewish cultural and communal life.

Elementary education was almost universal. However Jews suffered from humiliation and discrimination in grades given them. On the secondary and university level there was severe discrimination. Although the number of Jews studying in the high schools was high compared to the general Rumanian population, this can be partially explained by the greater opportunities for such education in the urban communities where most Jews lived and by their strong desire for a modern secular-type education. Many Jews from Rumania studied at universities abroad.

Marriage among Rumanian Jews was almost entirely endogamous. Jews married later than non-Jews and had fewer children.

During the early part of World War II Rumania was an ally of Nazi Germany and the situation of the Jews went from bad to worse. They were ejected from all segments of the economy, subjected to compulsory labor, and large numbers were systematically massacred. The economic exclusion of the Jews was accompanied by "legal" and illegal looting of property. In 1944, after Russian troops marched in, Rumania entered the war on the side of the Allies.

After the war the surviving Jews streamed back to their homes but very little was done by the authorities to restore Jewish property to its owners. When industry was nationalized in 1948 an estimated 100,000 Jews were left unemployed. The war was followed by a period of famine and starvation. Epidemics of spotted typhus and typhoid fever accompanied the droughts of 1945; tuberculosis was a severe threat to the population.

The Joint Distribution Committee (JDC) undertook a widespread program of health care and welfare for Rumanian Jewry. Together with OSE and ORT,[2] day-care centers, canteens and

[2] OSE is the somewhat abbreviated name for the *Union Mondiale pour la Protection de le Santé des Populations Juives et Oeuvres de Secours*

nurseries for infants, camps, hospitals, dispensaries, dental clinics, and medical centers were established. A survey by the JDC in the summer of 1947 revealed that 340,000 Jews, approximately 79 per cent of the total Jewish population, were on relief, with low incomes, or were in need of medical care. Since the activities of OSE and the JDC were so widespread, we may assume that many Rumanian Jews had experience with modern Western-oriented medical care during the immediate postwar period.

The anti-Jewish Rumanian government, through the Communist-dominated Jewish Democratic Committee, embarked on a policy aimed at repression of all religious, Zionist, or cultural activities of the Jewish community. By 1949 the JDC, ORT, and OSE offices were closed down and their institutions nationalized. Nineteen Jewish hospitals and 256 charity institutions were taken over by the state. Official reports of the Rumanian government state that health services have improved considerably since the war: there is a marked increase in the number of hospital beds and physicians per 1,000 inhabitants. However no information is available to enable us to judge the extent to which the Jewish population benefited from these general improvements in health services.

There were about 190,000 Jews in Rumania in the early 1950s. The Israeli census of 1961 reports that 127,340 people emigrated from Rumania to Israel after 1948, about three-quarters of them during the early 1950s and the remaining quarter after 1955.

POLISH IMMIGRANTS

Three periods are salient in the recent history of Polish immigration to Israel: the period preceding World War II, the period of World War II, and its aftermath. The majority of the Polish immigrants included in our study immigrated to Israel after 1956 and therefore spent several years in post-World-War-II Poland.

The pre-World-War-II period is marked by the establishment of Polish independence in 1919. Prior to that date the territories included in Poland had been partitioned in Russia, Austro-

---

aux Enfants; and ORT stands for Organization for Rehabilitation through Training.

Hungary, and Germany. At this time Poland signed a treaty with the Allied Powers in which she guaranteed the civil and political equality of the minority groups resident within her borders. In fact, however, the Polish government considered this treaty forced on her and never fully implemented it.

The old repressive laws and regulations against Jews which had existed before independence were not abolished. Jews were forbidden by local authorities to acquire land, were forced to pay special taxes for the care of their sick, many were not given citizenship, and few Jews were permitted to occupy government or municipal posts. Poland's long tradition of hatred and abuse of Jews resulted in the fact that pogroms were tolerated in a number of towns.

The Jewish population, which numbered somewhat over three million, lived largely in the towns: three-quarters of the Jews, as contrasted to one-quarter of the total Polish population, lived in towns of over 10,000 residents. They were employed in small industrial and commercial enterprises with heavy concentrations in the garment, leather, food, and printing industries as well as in watchmaking, jewelry, tinsmithing, and innkeeping. On the whole the Jews were extremely poor and only a very small percentage could be considered wealthy or even middle class. It is estimated that one-quarter to one-third of the Jews lacked any real means of subsistence during the 1930s. In fact there was substantial emigration of Jews from Poland during this period. Government control of economic life resulted in a great deal of discrimination against Jews. With the introduction of monopolies for match and tobacco production and the sale of salt, most Jews were eliminated from these fields.

Marriage was almost entirely endogamous even among the more assimilated segments of the Jewish population. The preferred marriage pattern, especially among Jews of means, was for a *talmid chacham*, a learned Jew. Learning was highly valued and a learned son-in-law brought prestige to the entire family. Marriage tended to be later than in the Polish population since Jews were more highly urbanized.

The Jews in Poland for centuries had carried on an active and well-organized communal life. There were autonomous regional and central organizations that fostered the development of religion, charity, education, as well as important economic, social, and political activities. The number of Jewish publications during the 1930s is an indication of a vigorous cultural life: there were thirty Yiddish dailies, five Polish language Jewish dailies, approximately 112 Yiddish weeklies, four Hebrew weeklies, and fourteen Polish-Jewish weeklies. Other periodicals included 137 printed in Yiddish, twenty-four in Hebrew, and fifty-five in Polish. Fifteen Yiddish theaters existed in Poland in 1936.

Jewish communal life also found expression in the political sphere. There were a large number of Jewish political parties representing all shades of opinion. They included a wide variety of Zionist parties, Aggudath Israel (religious), the Bund (Jewish Socialist party), and the Jewish Communists. In addition to their political activities these parties ran schools that taught both religious and secular subjects. The Zionist parties maintained schools in which Hebrew was the language of instruction, while the Bund supported Yiddish schools.

Attendance at primary school was compulsory in Poland. It can therefore be assumed that the majority of Jewish children received some form of secular education. In 1936–37 fully half of the Jewish children of school age were attending primary, secondary, or vocational schools run by Jewish authorities and about a fifth attended all-day Jewish schools. It is estimated that in the 1930s between 33 and 56 per cent of the boys of school age attended the traditional *heder*. Special restrictions and quotas were prevalent in the secondary schools and in institutions of higher learning so that students generally studied either in Jewish institutions or abroad. The relatively large number of Jewish university students who studied at near-starvation conditions abroad (about 8,000 in 1929) indicates the strong desire among Polish Jews for a secular education. The commitment to education is further reflected in the fact that almost half of the estimated sum spent for communal purposes was devoted to education.

The tradition of *bikur holim*, medical care and comfort for the sick, had been maintained in Polish Jewish communities for many generations. One estimate indicates that 4.7 per cent of the total communal expenditures during the 1930s were devoted to public health, which probably covered these activities. In 1922 TOZ, The Society for the Protection of Jewish Health, was founded in order to "guard the health of the broad Jewish masses, improve as far as possible their sanitary-hygienic conditions . . . and educate children in the modern hygienic manner" (Wulman, 1937, p. 7). Subventions were given to TOZ by local authorities and by the Ministry of Labor and Social Welfare, which apparently looked with favor on this organization. Its widespread influence during the 1930s is reflected in a speech delivered by the head of the Ministry of Health in 1933 in which he stated that ". . . today there is certainly not a single home in the country where it is not known what the three letters TOZ stand for" (Wulman, 1937, p. 77). By 1936 TOZ employed 243 physicians and thirty-five dentists in addition to a considerable auxiliary staff, and provided medical care at some thirty-eight outpatient clinics, twenty dentists' offices, twelve tuberculosis dispensaries and twenty-one well-baby stations. This organization stressed a social and preventive approach to medicine and carried on a program of health education that took the form of lectures and dissemination of popular booklets, leaflets and posters. Furthermore it cooperated with other Jewish organizations concerned with medicine and hygiene and assisted them in their work.

It is of considerable interest that during the 1930s about a third of all Polish physicians were Jews. Furthermore the infant and general mortality rates as well as the birth rate among Polish Jews were lower than the general population, despite the poverty in which most Jews lived. Against the background of general anti-Semitism referred to above, it may be surmised that Jews had comparatively easy access to their own physicians and health care institutions.

The period of World War II was characterized by a policy of wholesale extermination of Polish Jewry. Most of the three million Jews were killed in the death camps, the remainder were worked to death or starved in other camps or in the ghettos.

During the war, communal life was fundamentally disrupted. Nevertheless many communities managed, even in the face of extreme threats, to maintain certain elements of traditional activity. The policy of extermination was such, however, that the small num-

ber of survivors who remained in Poland at the time of the libera-
tion were characterized by extremely poor health, emaciation,
disease, and were in almost all cases without family members. It
has been estimated that a third of Polish Jewry after the war were
invalids, ill and unable to work.

The Jews who returned to their homes in Poland at the end
of the war generally found their houses and shops occupied by
Poles who had given the Jews up for lost and were generally quite
unprepared to relinquish their newly acquired property. A wave of
anti-Semitic violence began during this period and it was either impossible or dangerous for Jews to attempt to compete with the new
Polish shopkeepers. Furthermore in the immediate postwar period
the lack of raw materials as well as the high taxation made it virtually impossible for Jews to reopen their shops and businesses. A
sizeable number of Jews began to organize themselves into coopera-
tives which concentrated on such traditional Jewish occupations
as tailoring, shoemaking, and other crafts. With time Jews also
moved into heavy industry and into a variety of technical and professional occupations.

The survivors of Polish Jewry showed an immediate interest
in rebuilding Jewish life. It was as if they felt an obligation to renew
the cultural life destroyed by the Nazis. Despite widespread emigration, a real cultural revival was begun: an active attempt was
made to reestablish schools, children's homes, sanatoria, libraries, ·
publishing houses, choirs, cultural clubs, and religious welfare activities.

But this spurt of Jewish communal life was short-lived. In
1948 the Communists obtained a majority in the Polish government
and official policy toward Jews and Jewish institutions became
openly hostile. The government began to take over Hebrew and
Yiddish schools as well as Jewish welfare institutions. In 1950 the
Jewish Writers Association was dissolved; Jewish political parties
and Zionist youth groups were disbanded. In 1950 the Central
Jewish Committee was compelled to merge with the Communist-led
Jewish Cultural Society.

Although some elements of Jewish cultural life continue to
survive, there has been a strong tendency among Polish Jews, par-

ticularly the younger ones, to assimilate into the dominant Polish culture. There appears to be continued anti-Semitism, ranging from cases of discrimination in obtaining jobs or ostracizing Jewish children to physical violence and destroying of Jewish property.

The Polish government greatly expanded its health services after World War II. We may assume that Jews benefited along with non-Jews from these services. There is evidence of an improvement in the level of infant and general mortality although, as previously noted, these rates were for many years lower in the Jewish than in the non-Jewish population. During the postwar years health services were free to all segments of the population.

The overall impression gained from this brief survey is that Polish Jews come to Israel with a long tradition of positive attitudes toward health care and the medical profession. Their experience is of a relatively modern quality and their most recent encounters were with government-sponsored, bureaucratically organized medical services. Together with this tradition and experience it is important to bear in mind the traumatic impact of World War II on Polish Jewry and its particular relevance for their health and physical stamina.

It is also important to recall changes that occurred in Jewish cultural life before and after the war. The overall picture is one of a long tradition of extremely active and flourishing Jewish cultural life, dramatically interrupted and largely extinguished by the war, briefly revived immediately after the War, and then followed by a period of widespread assimilation and comparative quiescence of Jewish life as a result of official opposition to its development.

After 1948, when the state of Israel was founded, 115,530 Jews immigrated to Israel from Poland, about three-quarters of them during the early years of the state and the remaining quarter after 1955.

GROUPS IN THE STUDY

In order to round out this picture more fully we present some additional background data drawn from the respondents themselves, referring to their comparative age, education, occupation, level of religious observance, and size of family. It will be seen that these data complement the more general material presented above and serve to point up some differences among the groups studied.

Each of the immigrant groups in the study population arrived in Israel during a comparatively brief time span. Most of the urban Moroccans, urban and rural Kurds, and rural Rumanians arrived shortly after the state was established, between 1948 and 1951. The rural Moroccans and urban Poles are somewhat newer in the country, having immigrated after 1954. All of these groups are fairly homogeneous with respect to the period of arrival. Only the urban Rumanians are split into two subgroups: early arrivals who immigrated in 1950–51 and later arrivals who arrived in Israel after 1955.

There was nothing deliberate in our selection of the study populations in terms of these specific periods of immigration. Subjects were chosen in neighborhoods or villages in which concentrations of immigrants of the required ethnic origin who immigrated after 1948 were located: it would have been difficult to specify date of arrival more narrowly. However, this concentration of subjects in terms of period of arrival imposes a certain limitation on the analysis, specifically with respect to studying the process of acculturation: it is impossible to observe ethnic-residential groups in terms of the length of time they have been in the country. As a result we have resorted to a number of indirect methods, using substitute variables when they were meaningful.

The Moroccans and Kurds are younger on the average than the Europeans. Well over half of both non-European groups are under thirty-five years of age. The Rumanians are the oldest group and the urbans among them are particularly old with 34 per cent over the age of fifty-six. The urban Poles occupy a middle position with respect to age between the non-Europeans and the Rumanians.

As a whole the non-Europeans are characterized by a lower level of formal education than the Europeans. However, the urban Moroccans differ from the other non-Europeans in having attained a somewhat higher level of schooling: considerably fewer of them report no formal education at all. Among the Europeans there are virtually no cases of people who obtained no formal schooling but the Poles generally obtained a higher level of education than the Rumanians.

The picture with respect to occupation of the head of the household is parallel to that noted on educational level. The non-European groups are typically concentrated at the lower end of the occupational continuum largely in the skilled laborer and semi-skilled laborer categories. The Moroccans are somewhat higher than the Kurds, appearing more frequently in the skilled laborer category. Again the Poles show the highest concentration in the free professions and in other high-ranking jobs while the Rumanians fall between the Poles and non-Europeans in the level of their occupational status.

It does not appear to be coincidental that a striking parallel is to be found in the rank order of our ethnic groups on level of religious observance and the educational and occupational ordering. Taken as a whole, the non-Europeans are more observant than the Europeans, but among the non-Europeans we again find the urban Moroccans to be the least traditional group. Furthermore, the Poles in our population are the most secular-oriented while the Rumanians fall between the latter and the non-European groups.

The non-European families as a whole have more children than the Europeans. Practically none of the Europeans report more than six children while a substantial proportion of the non-Europeans do. Among the urban Kurds fully 45 per cent have over six children while 27 per cent of the urban Moroccans report this number, with the other non-European groups falling somewhere between these extremes.

These findings tend to confirm the ethnographic findings reported above concerning the transitional status which characterizes the Moroccans, in our case particularly the urbans in the Moroccan population studied. On several of the background variables they fall at a point on a continuum between the Kurds and the Europeans. This is true with respect to education, occupation, number of children in the family as well as level of religious observance. Such findings tend to confirm their middle position between the most traditional group observed (the Kurds) and the more westernized populations.

The differences noted among the ethnic groups included in the study point up the need to consider these background variables in any comparison of these groups undertaken in the course of the analysis. We have followed this procedure in testing the hypotheses and in other analyses which compare the groups.

PART TWO

ATTITUDES

4

Kupat Holim:
Patterns of
Utilization

In recent years the demands on medical facilities have increased considerably in most parts of the world. Technological advances in diagnosis and treatment require facilities for their exploitation and there is evidence of greater public appreciation of medical care. The rapid expansion of health insurance schemes has added to these demands (World Health Organization, 1965a; Feldstein, 1966). Frequency of utilization of health facilities in Israel has grown with this more general world trend and has reached a remarkably high level. This phenomenon has resulted in considerable public concern. In 1963–64 a special committee appointed by the Ministry of Health to consider the shortage of physicians devoted

61

special attention to the problem of high clinic utilization (Israel Ministry of Health, 1964).

This chapter examines the frequency of outpatient clinic use in Israel on a comparative basis in order to establish empirically the extent to which Israel differs from other countries. In addition the present chapter examines a number of correlates of utilization in an attempt to determine which subgroups in the population are the high utilizers.

FREQUENCY OF CLINIC USE

Over the past ten years, the average frequency of clinic use among Kupat Holim members has increased from 7.6 visits a year in 1956 to 8.7 visits a year in 1966. Up to 1962 there was a steady increase, reaching a peak of 9.1; since then there has been a small decline each year. The smaller sick funds, which insure almost a fifth of the population, show even higher rates of use and run as high as eleven visits per member a year (Israel Central Bureau of Statistics, 1967).

About two-thirds of these visits are to general practitioners (Kupat Holim, 1964). Nevertheless we will use the total attendance figure for the comparative analysis because data from other countries generally are not broken down by types of physicians visited.

There do not appear to be reliable analyses of the frequency of clinic use among subgroups of the Kupat Holim population broken down by age, sex, level of education, or income. The exception is a small study on frequency of visits undertaken by Kupat Holim in 1961. However, the limited scope of this study does not permit generalization (Kupat Holim, 1961). There is, however, evidence for differences in frequency of clinic use among various geographic regions of the country. Tel Aviv and Haifa show an average of over ten visits per member per year, while in the rural communities the figure is lower, reaching an average of six or seven visits per year (Kupat Holim, 1960).

The government committee referred to above stated that ten to twelve visits a year can be considered typical, taking into account some under-reporting by physicians (Israel Ministry of Health, 1964). Furthermore, this committee notes that the number of prescriptions per member per year may also be used as a relevant measure of utilization. One prescription per visit is considered reasonable. In England before 1952, when a charge for prescriptions was first levied, the annual number of prescriptions per patient was 6.07. In 1956 the figure went down to 5.1. In New Zealand it was 5.6; in Western Germany 6.4; in Austria 10.0. But in Israel the comparable figure is 18.0. Not only does Israel have a high absolute frequency of visits but the ratio of visits to prescriptions is also high (Martin, 1957).

Comparison of the Israel figures on clinic utilization to those of other countries requires that the comparable figures be drawn from schemes which are reasonably similar in terms of the structure and coverage of the services provided. In addition such schemes must be located in countries which have fairly similar morbidity rates. With these criteria in mind a number of insurance schemes were selected for comparison on frequency of utilization. These are listed in Table 1 with estimates of utilization rates as reported in the literature. It is clear that clinic attendance in Israel is in fact considerably more frequent than in these comparable medical insurance schemes. The only figures that are comparable are the higher estimates in certain of the East European countries but the lower estimates given there are considerably lower than the Israel figure. Most of the estimates range between three and five visits to the doctor per year—a figure which is substantially lower than the ten to twelve visits per year considered typical in Israel.

In an attempt to check whether frequency of attendance could be a function of a unique health or morbidity situation, we have compiled data on four general estimates of health level in the countries in which the various medical schemes are located. Table 2 presents data on the standardized mortality rate, infant mortality, population per doctor, and life expectancy at birth. While these are not the only variables which might be examined, they provide a reasonable estimate of the overall health situation. Examination of Table 2 indicates that Israel is comparatively well-off in terms of all four of these indices.

Some Israeli physicians actually feel that such high utilization rates may be a good thing—because of the more frequent and therefore better quality of medical care that high utilization provides: "Clinic attendance is always higher when clients have comprehensive insurance. This is a good thing from a medical point of view because we can catch early symptoms of illness."

But this point of view seems comparatively rare. Many of the physicians participating in our study expressed concern at what they considered over-utilization by members of Kupat Holim facilities. This is reflected in remarks made in the course of the discussion periods: "As one goes shopping for groceries several times a week, just so do they come to the Kupat Holim clinic. And if the queue isn't too long, they join it to see the doctor." "If I had a free subscription for soda water, wouldn't I stop by every kiosk for a drink? It doesn't cost anything to visit Kupat Holim so people come every day." "There are immigrant patients who come from Morocco or other countries where they never saw a doctor before in their lives. Here they get accustomed to coming to the clinic doctor every day, and sometimes more than once a day."

There is some awareness among Kupat Holim physicians that many patients come to the clinic for nonmedical reasons. While the specific latent functions were not referred to directly, physicians do indicate that some patients are not motivated only by concern with their health when they come to see the doctor. Although there is little spelling-out of what these motives might be, there is undoubtedly some awareness of their existence: "Lots of patients come not to get cured or to get rid of pain, but for quite different purposes." "New immigrants come to the doctor with all sorts of social problems." "In the immigrant communities, we find many patients who come for completely nonmedical reasons. Either they can't handle their economic problems or they feel unable to work. They start out going to the labor exchange, continue to the social welfare office, and land up in the clinic."

Many doctors feel that frequent utilization is often a result of a misunderstanding by uneducated clients of the principles of an insurance scheme: having paid their monthly premiums, clients demand to receive something for their money. Such an attitude is reflected in clients' statements that they have been paying regular premiums for months but have gotten nothing in return: "One patient said indignantly to me, 'I pay IL35 a month—and what for? I haven't seen a doctor for three months. Why shouldn't I come to the clinic?'" "Patients are always saying that they pay and

Table 1

FREQUENCY OF CLINIC UTILIZATION IN SELECTED MEDICAL
INSURANCE SCHEMES, 1950–1965

	Number of Visits per Year per Insured Person
National Health Services of:	
Britain[a]	3.1 — 7.2
Federal Republic of Germany[b]	5.0 — 8.0
Yugoslavia[c]	4.35 — 9.1
U.S.S.R.[d]	1.1 — 1.3
Czechoslovakia[e]	6.5 — 10.2
Netherlands Sick Fund System[f]	5.2
Windsor Medical Services (Canada)[g]	4.1
Kaiser Foundation Health Plan (U.S.A.)[h]	6.9
King Country Medical Service Corp. (U.S.A.)[i]	4.6
Bridge Clinic of Seattle, Washington (U.S.A.)[j]	4.0
Health Insurance Plan of Greater New York (U.S.A.)[k]	5.0 — 6.0

[a] Bierman *et al.,* 1968; Brotherston and Chave, 1956; Hill, 1951; Kedward, 1962; Logan, 1957; Stevenson, 1964; and Taylor, 1954.

[b] Hogarth, 1963.

[c] The lower estimate is taken from Vukmanovic, 1965. Vukmanovic also reports regional variations ranging from 2.52 in Montenegro to 6.19 in Slovenia. See also Silver, 1963b. The higher estimate is taken from Weber, 1965.

[d] Popon, 1962.

[e] The lower estimate is from a personal communication in May, 1966, by Dr. M. Vacek, Statistician, Vyzkumny Ustav Organisace Zdravotnictvi V Praze. The higher estimate is drawn from Weber, 1965. See also Logan and Eimerl, 1965.

[f] Our estimate is based on findings reported in Veldhoyzen Van Zanten, 1963.

[g] Darsky, Sinai, and Axelrod, 1958.

[h] Columbia University, 1962.

[i] Shipman, Lampman, and Miyamoto, 1962.

[j] Neiman, 1963.

[k] Health Insurance Plan of Greater New York, 1962; Anderson and Sheatsley, 1959.

Table 2

HEALTH STATUS OF COUNTRIES IN WHICH COMPARABLE INSTITUTIONS ARE LOCATED

	Standardized Mortality Rate[a]	Infant Mortality[b]	Population per Doctor[c]	Life Expectancy at Birth[a]
Israel: (Jewish Population)	5.92	24.1	390	M. 70.88 F. 73.01
Britain: England and Wales	6.51	21.4		M. 68.0 F. 73.9
N. Ireland	6.73	27.5	910	M. 67.6 F. 72.5
Scotland	7.48	25.8		M. 66.0 F. 71.9
Federal Republic of Germany	6.72	31.7	670	M. 66.8 F. 72.3

Yugoslavia	9.14	82.0	1400	M. 62.1 F. 65.2
USSR	—	32.0	500	70.0[c]
Czechoslovakia	6.97	22.7	550	M. 67.2 F. 72.8
Netherlands	5.37	15.4	890	M. 71.4 F. 74.8
Canada	6.22	27.2	860	M. 68.3 F. 74.1
U.S.A.	6.76	25.3	780	M. 66.6 F. 73.4

[a] Death rate per thousand. Standardized for 1962 Jewish population of Israel. Data from: World Health Organization, 1965b.
[b] World Health Organization, 1964.
[c] World Health Organization, 1964.
[d] United Nations, 1965.
[e] United Nations, 1964.

pay but never get anything for their money. They complain they are healthy and want to take advantage of service they've paid for."

Some physicians note the relationship of Kupat Holim to the larger institutional structure and see the source of high utilization rates in pressures imposed by other institutions. They feel that frequent clinic attendance is a result of demands made on clients in other parts of the social system: "The trouble is that every institution works on its own and there is no coordination among them. The social welfare office, and the police and the labor exchange— but each has no idea what the other is doing. We never even exchange information. If they would all work together there would be fewer clinic visits."

However, it is more common for physicians to place the blame for high utilization rates on the medical institution itself. They feel that the structure of the institution is such as to encourage clients to make repeated, frequently unnecessary, visits: through its inadequate system of receiving patients with little if any filtering, through its system of dispensing small quantities of drugs—ostensibly in an effort to prevent waste but in effect with the opposite result, namely that patients collect large amounts of unneeded drugs in their homes—and because of the ignorance of Kupat Holim patients who do not know what rights are due them under the insurance scheme. From this point of view it is the structure of the institution per se which encourages high utilization: "The *pakid* [reception clerk] just keeps admitting patients but has no idea what he's doing." "Why does Kupat Holim permit us to give prescriptions that last for only two or three days? As a result patients have to come again and again to renew their prescriptions." "If every Kupat Holim member were given a booklet explaining his rights and privileges, they wouldn't come so often. People don't know what they're entitled to."

The single solution referred to most frequently by the Kupat Holim physicians in the course of the discussion period concerned introduction of some sort of payment scheme for medical service. In many cases doctors noted that the payment should be small and symbolic. However, many expressed the feeling that payment, however small, would serve to reduce clinic utilization: "There will always be overuse of clinics as long as the service is free. We know that people take advantage of things they can get without cost." "There should be a charge for clinic visits or perhaps just for drugs. But certainly for visits to specialists. The charge should be graded for different income groups." "I once read an article that made the point that patients get well faster if they themselves pay for the doctor's care. It has a psychological influence on them." "Nothing will ever help—unless there is a charge for clinic visits."

It is worth noting that there has been some discussion of this possibility in the executive of Kupat Holim. Opinion is divided and feelings run high, especially since free access for members to medical service is a cardinal principle on which Kupat Holim has always been based. To change it would mean a major shift in the entire structure and ideology of the institution.

VALIDITY OF SELF-REPORTS

Official Kupat Holim data concerning frequency of clinic utilization are limited in scope and provide few, if any, social or attitudinal correlates of utilization. The present study, with its focus on sociological variables, made possible such an analysis. However, for this purpose systematic data on individual rates of clinic utilization are needed.

Kupat Holim records for individual subjects were found to be incomplete or unavailable at the time of our interview. Careful checking of records in several clinics convinced us that it would be impossible to obtain valid information on frequency of clinic attendance from the official Kupat Holim files. It was therefore decided early in the study to make use of information provided by the respondent.

The main problem in basing the analysis on self-reported frequency of utilization concerns the validity of such reporting. We consider this validity from two points of view. First, we survey reports in the literature on the general validity of morbidity or utilization data collected through sample surveys. Although our specific interest is in utilization rates, we have also noted research findings on validity or morbidity reported in field surveys. Second, we compare the reported frequency with other data on frequency of physician attendance in Kupat Holim.

The question posed in the course of the interview asked

about clinic attendance to all types of physicians—general practitioners as well as specialists—but did not include contacts with the clinic nurse.[1] It referred to a year-long, retrospective period in order to minimize the effects of seasonal variations and unique health conditions (Logan and Brooke, 1957). The average reported frequency in our population was 7.4 visits per person per year.[2]

Although some research has reported a reasonably high level of validity in reporting of illness and physician contacts in surveys (Anderson, Collette, and Feldman, 1963), the more general impression gained from the literature is of under-reporting: average reported frequencies are almost always lower than actual frequencies.[3] To some extent, this is a result of the memory factor (Collins, 1951; Downes and Mertz, 1953; Feldman, 1958; Gray, 1955; Logan and Brooke, 1957). It has also been noted that people tend to overestimate the favorableness of their own health (Suchman, Phillips, and Streib, 1958).

Other variables which have been shown to correlate with the validity of reporting illness in surveys are respondents' age (older people report with greater validity), recency of the physician contact (more recent contacts are more validly reported), and sex (females report with somewhat greater validity than males) (U.S. National Health Survey, 1965). Furthermore, the more serious the disease, and the more the respondent feels that it kept him from ordinary activities or left a defect, the more valid the reporting (Trussell and Elinson, 1959; Sanders, 1962). No differences in

---

[1] This is the same procedure as that followed in the HIP study (Health Insurance Plan of Greater New York, 1957). In the present study the question on which the frequency of attendance is based is worded as follows: "During the past year, how many times did you visit a Kupat Holim doctor because of your own health?" This wording attempted to eliminate such cases as mothers taking a child to a physician. Women attending for normal prenatal or postnatal care were counted separately.

[2] Computation of the mean frequency of clinic attendance was based on midpoints of the categories used in the question (see footnote 1 above). In the last category, "20 or more," we used 20 as the estimate for calculating the mean—a conservative procedure which tends to lower our mean.

[3] Under-reporting is described in: Elinson and Trussell, 1957; Health Insurance Plan of Greater New York, 1957; Simmons and Bryant, 1962; U.S. National Health Survey, 1961; and Feldman, 1960. Validity in survey data is discussed by Belloc, 1954; and by Solon, Sheps, Lee, and Barbano, 1962.

validity of reporting appear by race, education, or income (U.S. National Health Survey, 1965).

It is of some interest that in one study it was found that only 64 per cent of those who saw a doctor during the two-week period prior to the interview reported this fact at the time of the interview (U.S. National Health Survey, 1965). A similar finding is that HIP members reported 3.5 physician contacts a year in a survey while HIP records for the same period showed 5.3 physician contacts. This represents under-reporting by a third (Health Insurance Plan of Greater New York, 1957).

What is of particular relevance to our analysis is the finding that frequency of actual physician contact during the previous year is positively related to validity in reporting. In one study it is reported that among those who had ten or more physician contacts during the previous year, 88 per cent reported this fact accurately when interviewed. The figure for those with fewer contacts is considerably lower (U.S. National Health Survey, 1965). Such a finding suggests that in using survey data we would do better to focus on the subgroup reporting high frequency of doctor attendance. This is the course we have followed.

The overall impression from the literature surveyed indicates that there is generally under-reporting of attendance. This under-reporting is differentially distributed in the population in terms of a number of background characteristics and in terms of the nature of the illness experienced. But those who, in an interview situation, report high frequency of physician attendance are more likely to be reporting validly than those who report low attendance.

The major difficulty in comparing the reported frequency of physician attendance with official Kupat Holim figures stems from the fact that the population in our survey is aged twenty years and over, while Kupat Holim figures refer to the total insured population. Official Kupat Holim figures do not present utilization data in terms of the age of the insured population so that some difficulty is encountered when we attempt to determine the official rates for the comparable age group. The best we have been able to come up with is an approximation. Since the data for the present study were collected during 1961 and 1962, the comparison with Kupat Holim figures will focus on those years.

Kupat Holim reports that its members visited a physician on the average of about nine times in 1962 and 1963. The youngest children are known to be high attenders while older children and youth are low attenders. The average physician attendance for the population under five, who comprise about one-tenth of the total membership, is 11.27 per year.[4] The age group between five and nineteen visits infrequently (Brotherston and Chave, 1956; Cohen et al., 1967; Sa'adia, 1965), but this group comprises about a third of the Israeli population (Israel Central Bureau of Statistics, 1961). These two opposite patterns, and the larger proportion of the five-to-nineteen age group, results in a lower average frequency for the total Kupat Holim population than for the population aged twenty and over. If we were to eliminate insured persons under the age of twenty, it would seem safe to assume that the average number of clinic visits a year would be over nine.

What may we therefore conclude concerning the average of 7.4 reported visits per member per year which we obtained in our survey? In view of the research findings concerning validity of such reporting and the fact that we have confined ourselves to people twenty years old and over, our figure would seem reasonable to represent the typical underestimate of the actual frequency for the comparable age group. If we assume that the "true" frequency of the group aged twenty and over is nine or more, our figure of 7.4 represents an underestimate of about one-third or a quarter. This seems to correspond to the findings of other research.

CORRELATES OF UTILIZATION

In light of the findings reported above concerning the greater validity of reporting by high utilizers, we have chosen to present the analysis in terms of the subgroup characterized by the highest reported frequency of physician attendance. This subgroup reports twenty or more physician contacts a year.[5] If we

---

[4] Communicated by S. Seligson-Singer of the Division of Medical Statistics, Kupat Holim. The proportion of children under four years old in the *total* Israel population in 1960 was 12.4 per cent (see Israel Central Bureau of Statistics, 1961).

[5] Our question was worded to refer to the number of times a respondent went to the clinic and did not include home visits by the doctor which

assume general under-reporting of physician contacts, we can assume that this group undoubtedly represents the high utilizers, since they visit the physician at least twenty times a year. Furthermore this probably represents a conservative estimate since the category used in the interview was "twenty visits or more" a year; some of the respondents included in this subgroup therefore reported visiting their physician *more* than twenty times.[6] In order to make sure that a cutting point of twenty or more visits was not exaggeratedly high, the entire analysis was also done on the group reporting ten or more visits a year. The findings are identical to those reported on the more extreme group.

The following correlates were examined: ethnicity, place of residence, sex, age, religiosity, knowledge of Hebrew, present and former use of traditional medical practitioners, level of education, and number of children.

Of the total surveyed population, 16 per cent report twenty or more visits a year to the Kupat Holim physician. (A similar percentage report that they visit the Kupat Holim nurse twenty or more times a year: 14 per cent). Our findings reveal no consistent patterning in terms of ethnicity or place of residence. The urban Kurds show the highest frequency of attendance while the urban Poles show the lowest. But there is no evidence for systematic differences between the European and non-European groups or between the urban and rural groups.

The above findings differ from certain other reported findings in Israel. Sa'adia (1965) found in a study of a new immigrant urban practice that among adults up to the age of sixty, Kupat Holim members of Asian-African origin have more contacts with

---

average less than .5. We did not feel that it would be practical or feasible to have respondents distinguish between visits that were limited only to questions or other brief contacts and longer visits involving actual diagnosis or treatment. See Lees and Cooper, 1963.

[6] Our procedure parallels Silver's (1963a), who defines high utilizers as those who utilize more than twice the median number of services of the family physician. Twenty visits a year in Israel also represents about twice the mean annual number of visits. The procedure is the same although the mean or median rate of utilization in Silver's study was approximately half the Israeli figure.

the physician than European members. He does not specify the precise country of origin of his respondents, but groups them together as "Asian-Africans."

Many of the physicians themselves seem to have the impression that immigrants from Asian and African countries are high clinic utilizers. One gains the feeling in the course of the discussion periods that this notion is widespread among the doctors: "People from Asian and African countries come to the doctor more frequently, especially for small ailments." If, in the present study, we were to combine the urban and rural Moroccans and Kurds into one group, their frequency of clinic attendance would also be higher than that of the Europeans. Our findings point to the importance of looking at specific ethnic groups in greater detail.

Other studies of rural clinics in Israel show a considerably lower frequency of physician contact than our data indicate. Reporting on a rural Kurdish village, Cohen et al. (1967) found 1.6 visits for males and 2.5 visits for females per year in 1960. Our average for the rural Kurds is 6.7 contacts a year. The same study reports on two Moroccan villages in which the average number of physician contacts for males was 2.9 and 3.4 while for females in the same villages the figures were 4.1 and 5. In our study we found 7.9 visits per year among rural Moroccans. Wamoscher (1964) found an average of 4.1 contacts a year in rural Moshavim.

We are unable to state unequivocally why the attendance figure in our study is so much higher than that found by the other researchers cited. It is worth recalling the probable under-reporting in our data, which would mean that the figures cited in our study should really be even higher. One relevant fact concerning our rural populations is that in all cases there was a Kupat Holim clinic in the specific rural community even though patients were not always received daily. In the case of Cohen et al. (1967) a "practical nurse" was resident in the village but the physician was available only at a center. Furthermore, the authors report that the number of physician contacts decreases with the distance of the village from the regional clinic. This suggests that our high figure could be associated with the fact that the clinics were located in the village proper (Purola et al., 1968).

Comparatively high frequency of physician contacts is found

among women, older respondents, more religious people, respondents who know less Hebrew, respondents who now use or formerly used traditional practitioners, larger families, and people with less formal education (Table 3). The findings are almost entirely consistent for all of the ethnic and residential groups; we have tested the relationships for independence and the data indicate that all of them hold for every combination of two variables. In order to be certain that a higher illness rate among these subgroups is not the motivating factor in the utilization patterns described, we have also controlled for respondents' self-reported health status. Respondents were asked to define themselves as "very sick," "fairly sick," "somewhat sick," "fairly healthy," or "very healthy." Again we find that the relationships described hold consistently.

The overall impression gained from our data is that high utilization is concentrated principally among the less acculturated, lower-class subgroups: the former consists of the older, female, non-Hebrew speaking, more religious, and more traditional parts of the population, while the latter consists of the less educated people with larger families.

Other research in Israel (Cohen et al., 1967; Sa'adia, 1965; Wamoscher, 1964) has shown a similar pattern of utilization for sex and age groups, with women and older adults showing higher frequencies of physician contacts. Sa'adia also reports a positive relationship between frequency of physician contact and length of time the immigrant is in Israel: old-timers in his study show more contact than newer arrivals. Our study did not permit a systematic examination of the relationship between utilization and length of time in the country. However, we did observe the relationship of physician contact to knowledge of Hebrew and current or past use of traditional medical practitioners—which can be thought of as "acculturation" variables and roughly analogous to a measure of time in Israel. Our findings show a picture reversed from the one noted by Sa'adia: respondents who know less Hebrew and who used or continue to utilize traditional medical practitioners are comparatively frequent utilizers of the Kupat Holim physician. These represent the less acculturated subgroup of the population.

Sa'adia's findings do not show a clear relationship between physician contacts and size of family. In our study, the larger

Table 3

PERCENTAGE REPORTING 20 OR MORE PHYSICIAN CONTACTS A YEAR

Background Variables	Urban Moroccans	Rural Moroccans	Urban Kurds	Rural Kurds	Urban Rumanians	Rural Rumanians	Urban Poles
Sex							
Men	9 (137)	14 (140)	21 (123)	9 (138)	15 (138)	5 (157)	5 (125)
Women	11 (168)	18 (124)	39 (128)	29 (111)	22 (125)	17 (122)	11 (110)
Age							
Under 35	7 (184)	13 (140)	28 (126)	11 (148)	— (27)	— (72)	12 (41)
36 and over	13 (118)	19 (124)	33 (125)	28 (99)	20 (233)	14 (207)	7 (194)
Religiosity							
Less Traditional	7 (120)	4 (47)	14 (51)	13 (88)	14 (184)	8 (232)	6 (215)
More Traditional	12 (183)	18 (217)	35 (200)	20 (164)	28 (79)	23 (47)	25 (20)

Knowledge of Hebrew							
Good Knowledge	6 (166)	5 (74)	16 (88)	7 (96)	4 (67)	5 (115)	4 (114)
Poor Knowledge	11 (186)	20 (181)	39 (161)	24 (150)	23 (196)	14 (164)	11 (121)
Use of Traditional Practitioner							
Never used	9 (227)	8 (144)	28 (179)	9 (140)	17 (182)	9 (208)	9 (208)
Use now or once used	12 (76)	31 (120)	35 (72)	29 (107)	30 (57)	16 (70)	16 (70)
Number of Children							
3 or less	10 (127)	12 (76)	19 (64)	15 (85)	15 (223)	10 (240)	7 (216)
4 or more	10 (164)	18 (181)	35 (177)	37 (84)	54 (22)	24 (25)	18 (11)
Education of Head of Household							
Completed 8 grades or more	8 (153)	13 (45)	19 (62)	11 (44)	12 (59)	7 (123)	7 (184)
Did not complete 8 grades	14 (148)	17 (219)	34 (189)	19 (204)	27 (109)	13 (156)	8 (49)

the family, the more frequent the contact with the physician. Furthermore, we find inverse relationship between level of education and utilization. Both size of family and level of education can be taken as rough estimates of social class.

SUMMARY

We have shown that frequency of clinic attendance in Israel is greater than in countries having comparable medical insurance schemes. This high frequency, which is estimated to range between ten and twelve clinic visits a year per insured person, does not appear to be accounted for by high morbidity rates.

Since it was necessary to base the analysis of clinic attendance on frequencies reported by the respondents themselves, we first looked into the validity of such self-reported data. The literature indicates that the general trend is one of under-reporting. Such under-reporting is differentially distributed among people who have experienced different diseases as well as among men and women and among respondents of varying ages. The recency of the illness experience as well as its seriousness also play a role in the completeness of reporting in an interview situation. What is most important for the present purposes is the finding concerning the positive relationship between frequency of physician utilization and validity of its reporting: the most frequent utilizers are apparently the most valid reporters. This finding led us to base our analysis of the correlates of utilization on the group with self-reported high physician attendance.

When we compared the average of 7.4 visits a year reported by the population studied here with figures from official Kupat Holim sources as well as from a number of field surveys carried out in Kupat Holim clinics, we found about the expected level of under-reporting, namely an underestimate of about one-third or one-fourth.

Taking the group with a self-reported frequency of twenty or more visits to the physician a year as our focus, a number of background correlates were examined. The analysis suggests that high utilization is concentrated among the less acculturated, lower-class subgroup which is probably in less contact with the mainstream of Israeli life, that is, the older, female, non-Hebrew speaking, more religious, more traditional segments of the population characterized by a lower level of education and by larger families.

Higher morbidity rates alone probably would not be sufficient to explain this pattern. Furthermore we have demonstrated that these relationships hold among self-defined sick as well as healthy people. It would therefore seem reasonable to surmise that certain sociological or psychological aspects of the immigration process may be playing a part in this configuration. We would suggest that the greater the ambiguity and the ambivalence which confront the immigrant and the less he feels capable of providing solutions on his own, the more likely he may be to seek such solutions within the framework of the medical institution. There is a suggestion from these data that persons who have not yet entered fully into the mainstream of Israeli life or who may feel its pressures unduly because of their low socioeconomic position, may seek to cope with the many problems that confront them through illness.

The leveling off or lowering of the utilization rates among the relatively more acculturated group could be explained by at least two possible processes: (1) resolution of many of the early problems through time alone or through the mechanism of illness so that the need for the institution is reduced. This could mean that Kupat Holim may in fact be playing a functional acculturative role, which is, actually, one of its goals (Kanev, 1965). It is certainly of some interest to recall that official Kupat Holim utilization rates show a peak figure in 1962 and a slow decline after that date. By this date immigration was greatly reduced and many of the earlier arrivals were well on their way in the advancing acculturation process. (2) A focusing on other social mechanisms as potential aids in problem resolution. This could imply a growing recognition by clients that Kupat Holim in fact does *not* play the expected role, or it could mean a greater acquaintance with alternative institutional or personal mechanisms which play a parallel role for the more acculturated immigrant.

5

Defining Oneself as Ill

The paradigm of the hypotheses to be tested makes systematic use of a variable called *the tendency to define oneself as ill*. This variable, in combination with each of the needs, defines the critical group which, we predict, will be most likely to seek satisfaction of the need through the latent functions of the medical institution. It will be recalled that the rationale behind the inclusion of this variable concerns its "filtering" role in directing Kupat Holim members toward the medical institution rather than toward other institutional contexts as a potential satisfier of their needs. We proposed that Kupat Holim would play a more salient role in the general orientation of people with a high tendency to define themselves as ill and they would therefore be more likely than others to select it as an appropriate alternative for need satisfaction.

In view of the central role of this tendency variable in our analysis, we have devoted a brief chapter to it in an attempt to shed some light on the role it is likely to play in terms of its correlates. Among the latter we will consider respondents' ethnic origin, rural-urban residence, age, sex, level of education, extent of religious orthodoxy, and level of knowledge of Hebrew. Length of time in Israel could not be systematically considered because there was very little variation on this variable within the ethnic groups since each immigrated within a short time span. We have limited the analysis in this chapter to the above demographic correlates since relationships to a variety of attitudinal variables are considered in other chapters of the study.

Mechanic (and Volkart, 1960, 1961) in their discussion of the tendency to adopt the sick role, have pointed to the importance of subjective as well as objective factors in determining just when people consider themselves eligible to enter this role and have noted that "not all organically 'sick' people define themselves as ill" (see also Kasl and Cobb, 1966; Rosenstock, 1966; Zola, 1964). The same symptoms will motivate one person to visit his doctor while another will either ignore the symptoms, wait and see what happens, or perhaps not even define them as requiring professional care (Koos, 1954).

From the individual's point of view, the sick role offers a number of secondary gains to its incumbents so that being sick is not necessarily a situation to be avoided. Consciously or unconsciously, some people may actually want to be sick in order to gain certain of the latent rewards of illness. For such people illness is often an attractive role.

But this tendency is not entirely an individual matter; it may be group-conditioned by collectively held norms. In one group, it may be that preventive, that is, presymptomatic, action is stressed; in another, ambiguous symptoms which give no "real trouble" will be regarded as justification for seeking medical care; in a third, only functional incapacitation is seen as requiring professional medical attention.

We have followed Mechanic's lead in defining the tendency to enter the sick role by means of an ambiguous set of symptoms which were presented to the respondent as hypothetical situations. He was asked to state how he would respond if he had the following symptoms: a persistent cold and running nose without temperature, a bad cough without temperature, a temperature of 38° but no other symptoms. Alternative answers ranged from "I wouldn't do anything," "I would wait for it to pass," to "I would go to see the doctor," "I would ask the doctor to come to my home." Those giving the latter type of response were defined as high in the tendency to define themselves as ill, while those who reported that they would be likely to ignore or do little about such symptoms were defined as low on the tendency.[1]

Our data show that ethnic origin is a definite factor in conditioning the tendency to adopt the sick role. As a whole, the non-Europeans, both Moroccans and Kurds, display a greater tendency than the Europeans to enter the sick role. The differences between the Europeans and the non-Europeans hold when other variables are introduced as controls: even the European subgroups with a relatively high tendency only rarely reach the level of any of the comparable non-European subgroups in the frequency with which they define themselves as ill. And conversely: even the non-European groups wtih the lowest tendency—for example, the best educated subgroups—are generally higher than any European subgroup. The evidence suggests that this is a normative pattern of these cultural groups.

There are other research findings on the high tendency of Jews, as compared to other groups, to adopt the sick role. Zborowski (1952, 1969) has shown that Jews and Italians tend to exaggerate pain experience. Mechanic (1963) has demonstrated that Jews are high in the tendency to enter the sick role. In a study of sociomedical variations among a number of ethnic groups, Suchman (1964, 1965a) has shown that Jews are comparatively high in acceptance of the sick role as well as in preventive medical behavior. His analysis is based on a Jewish population of European origin in New York City, while our data permit a differentiated approach to subgroups of Jews with varying cultural backgrounds. We do not have non-Jewish groups available for comparison, but the data presented here indicate that there may be wide differences among

---

[1] The four items were dichotomized and were found to define a Guttman scale. R = .91.

the Jews themselves when a more detailed breakdown of this overall group is possible.

During the group discussions many physicians referred to the high propensity of Jews to visit doctors. Jews are often viewed by the doctors themselves as characterized by a tendency to worry excessively about their health and to visit a physician for the slightest symptom: "Jews are always more concerned about their health." "Did you ever hear the story of the Englishman, the Pole, and the Jew who were thirsty? The Englishman asked for tea, the Pole ordered a bottle of vodka, and the Jew rushed to his doctor to find out if he is not diabetic." "Whoever the doctor, you'll always find that the majority of his patients are Jews. Jews like to take care of their health."

Tables 4 and 5 show the role of the other independent variables within the ethnic groups. On the whole, we find a greater tendency to enter the sick role among women than among men, among older than younger people, among less educated than better educated,[2] among religious- than among secular-oriented respondents,[3] among immigrants who know little Hebrew than among those who already know the language. These trends emerge most clearly among Moroccans, both urban and rural, but less consistently in the other groups. The urban Poles show few variations among the subgroups observed.

The tendency to enter the sick role appears to be concentrated among people who are less sophisticated, less knowledgeable about disease and its implications, and who therefore seek out the expert physician to deal with ambiguous symptoms. This syndrome appears to be the one Knupfer (1953) refers to when she describes

[2] It is of some interest to note that Koos (1954) makes the point that upper-class people go to a physician more frequently both for minor and for serious symptoms. In this case, in which we are dealing only with apparently minor symptoms, the opposite is the case. The availability and accessibility of the clinic are undoubtedly relevant. See also Mechanic, 1963, p. 204.

[3] Mechanic (1963) proposes that church attendance would be inversely related to the tendency to visit a physician. Due to small numbers of cases in his subgroups, the statistical test available to him is weak. Our findings, however, show the opposite to be the case in most of the ethnic-residential groups and in some groups there is no relationship.

Table 4

Tendency to Enter the Sick Role (Percentage) by Sex, Age, and Education

	Sex		Age			Education of Head of Household	
	Men	Women	Under 35	36–45	Over 46	Did not complete 8 grades	Completed 8 grades or more
Urban Moroccans	57 (135)	72 (136)	54 (186)	56 (78)	74 (39)	63 (146)	52 (159)
Rural Moroccans	63 (140)	74 (143)	69 (157)	64 (83)	74 (43)	74 (223)	58 (50)
Urban Kurds	73 (123)	72 (130)	72 (127)	65 (68)	81 (58)	73 (189)	70 (64)
Rural Kurds	64 (138)	69 (123)	66 (157)	67 (45)	67 (57)	67 (214)	61 (46)
Urban Rumanians	36 (136)	48 (123)	48 (25)	33 (57)	44 (174)	42 (105)	41 (153)
Rural Rumanians	31 (156)	35 (122)	32 (72)	29 (86)	37 (120)	34 (155)	31 (123)
Urban Poles	45 (119)	56 (109)	47 (43)	46 (90)	45 (96)	38 (47)	47 (180)

Table 5

TENDENCY TO ENTER THE SICK ROLE (PERCENTAGE) BY RELIGION AND LANGUAGE

	Religious Identification			Hebrew		
	Very Orthodox	Somewhat Orthodox	Secular	Speaks, reads, and writes fluently	Speaks but does not read and write fluently	Speaks haltingly or not at all, does not read and write
Urban Moroccans	65 (94)	50 (90)	57 (122)	49 (94)	57 (136)	68 (75)
Rural Moroccans	70 (141)	77 (79)	60 (55)	50 (40)	60 (86)	78 (148)
Urban Kurds	76 (144)	62 (56)	74 (53)	73 (33)	72 (94)	76 (120)
Rural Kurds	70 (107)	67 (66)	61 (88)	61 (54)	61 (85)	72 (119)
Urban Rumanians	44 (39)	42 (38)	41 (182)	37 (35)	31 (103)	52 (121)
Rural Rumanians	60 (10)	41 (37)	30 (231)	25 (57)	31 (134)	40 (87)
Urban Poles	50 (8)	27 (11)	46 (210)	49 (74)	39 (94)	51 (61)

people who feel "less competent to judge." She notes that such persons "will leave decisions to wiser men," in this case the physician. Since there is pressure to resolve ambiguity and people with the characteristics described probably feel less competent to do so on their own, they will turn to an expert to resolve it for them by interpreting the symptoms within some sort of meaningful frame of reference. Better informed, more sophisticated people will feel more competent to resolve the ambiguity by themselves (Kadushin, 1964; Levine, 1962). Analysis of utilization patterns showed a similar patterning, with lower-class, less acculturated groups showing comparatively high rates (see Chapter Four). It will be recalled that we suggested that this pattern is associated with the process of immigration.

These findings contrast with results of surveys in the United States, which show lower-class people to be characterized less by a tendency to adopt the sick role (King, 1962; Shostak and Gomberg, 1964). The general availability and accessibility of the Kupat Holim clinic in Israel serves as a background factor to this very different pattern. Since the doctor is available and one has the right to seek his services without cost, people who are not well informed about the meaning of symptoms or their possible consequences, feel that any symptom, even the slightest, should be attended by him. In such a situation, one has to be fairly certain that the symptom is medically insignificant in order not to enter the sick role. Such certainty is more characteristic of better informed people.

The fact that all of the non-European groups show a higher tendency than the Europeans to enter the sick role is striking. Tables 4 and 5 show that even the younger, better educated, more secular oriented, and more expert in Hebrew among the non-Europeans reveal a more frequent tendency to define themselves as ill. Such a pattern suggests a more general ethnic norm which operates over and above the differences noted among specific subgroups defined by age, education, religiosity, or knowledge of Hebrew.

It is difficult to judge whether the empirical pattern observed here has been transferred by these ethnic groups from their countries of origin or whether it is a response to the specific Israeli situation. On the whole, people from non-European countries had less experience with Western-type medicine and with the interpretation of symptoms within its framework. While a European with fairly long experience with Western medical practice feels enough confidence in his own ability at self-diagnosis of minor symptoms, the non-European may seek out professional authority under the same circumstances. In addition non-Europeans have had less experience with prepayment schemes. The knowledge that they have already paid for the service could motivate them to want to utilize it even for relatively minor symptoms, in an effort to "get their money's worth."

The similarity of the findings in this chapter to those reported in the analysis of clinic utilization needs to be borne in mind when the hypotheses are tested. We have shown that lower-class, less acculturated, less sophisticated subgroups of the population are more frequent clinic attenders and are more likely to show a high tendency to define themselves as ill. Frequency of clinic utilization appears as a dependent variable in much of the subsequent analysis while the tendency serves to define the basic typology which is the major independent variable in testing the hypotheses. Therefore, when the number of cases in the subgroups permit detailed analysis, we have consistently examined the relationships based on these variables with controls on ethnicity, sex, age, and education.

PART THREE

LATENT
FUNCTIONS

6

Setting for Catharsis

The idea is widespread that, over and above the need for specific diagnosis or treatment of illness, people come to the doctor in order to talk, gain a sympathetic ear and take advantage of his ostensible willingness to listen to them. Sanders (1963) refers specifically to this willingness as a latent function of the health system.

The manifest functions of the medical institution in fact require the physician to devote a certain amount of time and effort to listening in his attempt to cure or prevent illness. Ideally this listening should be carried out in a sympathetic, supportive, and noncritical spirit. Insofar as the patient is concerned, he is expected to bring only medical problems to the clinic and not to discuss medically irrelevant matters in his encounter with the physician.

The latent function of the medical institution in this area emerges because of the ambiguity of the definition of a medical problem. The boundaries between medical and nonmedical problems have become increasingly blurred in recent years as the medical profession comes to view the individual in his wider social

91

context. As more and more factors in the patient's background and social environment become relevant to diagnosis and prevention, it becomes increasingly difficult for the physician to decide that subjects brought up by the patient should not be considered and listened to with professional attention. There is therefore a certain pressure on the physician to categorize subjects brought up as medical rather than nonmedical. Although this comprehensive point of view is not accepted fully by all physicians, it probably represents a growing trend.

The latent function appears when people with marginally medical or nonmedical problems take advantage of the physician's availability as a sympathetic listener. Another form of exploitation can occur when people with a legitimate medical problem talk and discuss it more than is necessary. We have seen that it is increasingly difficult for the modern physician to limit or block such exploitation.

The need for a sympathetic, supportive listener might be greatest among immigrants who have undergone social changes which accentuate their isolation. We refer to the breakdown of the extended family system, particularly among tradition-oriented non-Europeans. Such a process of change could leave members with an increased sense of detachment and isolation until other ties are cemented or substitute mechanisms developed. Another source of isolation which impinges on immigrants is the settlement policy, which often places them in mixed ethnic communities. The problem of communication among culturally differentiated subgroups of the population could contribute to the individual's sense of aloneness. In addition, the material and emotional problems which accompany the integration and acculturation processes might heighten the individual's need for a sympathetic, understanding, noncritical ear (Balint, 1966). For all of these reasons, we might expect immigrants to take advantage of this latent function of the medical institution. At the same time it is important to note that loneliness as well as a need for sympathy and support exist in all societies although prevalence may vary.

Of course the reality of the doctor-patient relationship can be quite different from its ideal structuring. We know that the medical bureaucracy in which Kupat Holim physicians work may impede some aspects of his ideal role performance. The requirement to receive a specific number of patients per hour, the burden of paper work, and the paucity of secretarial assistance may result in a minimum of time to devote to each patient. With such time pressure, only those physicians most committed to the ideal role pattern will be able to provide patients with substantial amounts of support, sympathy, and understanding. This problem is not necessarily limited to the salaried physician practicing in a bureaucratic medical structure. Other pressures, for example economic considerations, could produce similar results in the care of the private solo practitioner.

Furthermore, although the more comprehensive view of the professional role has been widely accepted in the profession, it has not been internalized fully by all physicians. Some doctors, perhaps as a rationalization of the above noted bureaucratic pressures or possibly because of their own perception of the professional role, do not view this function as part of their own role pattern. Such physicians would tend to define their professional orientation in more specific terms and to believe that patients who want to talk in order to gain support and sympathy should go to a psychiatrist rather than to a general practitioner.

OVERVIEW OF VARIABLES

The need for catharsis is defined in terms of a set of questions which inquire whether the individual feels that he has enough people to whom he can talk freely and who listen to him with sympathy and understanding. These questions were formulated as follows: Do you know enough people with whom you feel free to talk about your personal problems? Do you sometimes feel that people around you are so rushed and busy that they never have a chance just to sit down and talk or chat? Do you sometimes feel when you are chatting with friends or acquaintances that they are paying no attention to you?[1]

It is interesting that the differences among our ethnic groups

[1] Dichotomizing each of these items yielded a Guttman scale. R = .93. The scale continuum was divided for purposes of the analysis into respondents with a greater need for catharsis and respondents with a lesser need for catharsis.

on this variable are small despite the considerable cultural differences among them: approximately a third express a high need for catharsis. We do not find evidence that the more traditional groups feel a greater need for catharsis than the others.

Furthermore a more detailed analysis of the ethnic groups in terms of sex, age, and education categories does not reveal any systematic trends. We might have expected, for example, that older non-Europeans, who grew up in the context of extended family systems, would find themselves comparatively isolated, especially in the urban centers, and would therefore express a comparatively high need for catharsis. The data do not indicate this to be the case. It would therefore seem that different backgrounds of family structure do not play much of a role in determining the current level of need for catharsis.

We have observed two dimensions of need satisfaction with respect to catharsis. One, in the more classic sense, concerns the physician as potential satisfier of the catharsis need. The other concerns the nurse in this role.

We have already discussed the physician's role as potentially satisfying patients' need for catharsis. The inclusion of the nurse as provider of catharsis is based on the definition of her professional role which requires "understanding" and "total patient care" as standard professional performance (MacGregor, 1965). What is more, she may, in some cases, provide for this need when the physician, for whatever reason, fails to. This could represent a "spillover" of the doctor's role to another member of the medical team: when patients fail to obtain sympathy and understanding from the doctor, they may try to get it from the nurse. Moreover, her social class position is closer to that of many clients and could encourage such a "spillover." The lesser status-gap might work to increase rapport between nurse and patient (Simmons, 1955, 1958a). In some cases the nurse may even be anxious to take over certain of the physician's ideal functions as a means of emphasizing her full medical competence.

It is an empirical question whether nurses do in fact provide for the catharsis need; the opposite trend of refusing to provide sympathy and understanding, because of work load or narrow role definition, could also occur.

THE PHYSICIAN

We have defined the client's perception of the physician as satisfying the need for catharsis by means of the following questions: After you have visited the Kupat Holim doctor, do you generally feel good as a result of having talked over your problems freely with him? Do you generally manage to talk with your Kupat Holim doctor about problems that are difficult or awkward for you to discuss with others? When you tell your Kupat Holim doctor about your illness, do you find that he often tells you that you are just complaining about nothing? The same items were repeated, substituting *nurse* for *doctor*. Two Guttman scales were defined by dichotomizing these items.

In Table 6, we can compare the ethnic groups on their perception of the Kupat Holim physician as satisfier of the need for catharsis. The most frequent failure to satisfying this need through the doctor is expressed by the Rumanians. Although the difference is not large, it is statistically significant. Further analysis shows that the Rumanians' dissatisfaction is concentrated more among the younger members of this group who apparently fail more frequently to satisfy their need for catharsis with the physician. The same trend is found among the Moroccans. Other than these differences, we do not find any meaningful trends in the analysis of the subgroups.

THE NURSE

Table 6 does not indicate that the nurse satisfies clients' need for catharsis more frequently than the doctor; the physician is more often perceived as sympathetic, understanding, and supportive. While the differences are not large, they are systematic and there is no suggestion that this function has been shifted to the nurse, although she also plays a role in satisfying clients' need for catharsis. Judging by clients' reports, it therefore appears that both doctor and nurse fulfill this role, with the physician performing it somewhat more frequently.

There is a small but significant tendency for Moroccans and Kurds to report greater satisfaction of the catharsis need through the Kupat Holim nurse while European groups report such satisfaction somewhat less frequently. This finding is consistent with the proposal that nurses tend to provide satisfaction of the need for catharsis for clients for whom the status-gap to the physician is large.

There is a suggestion, although it is not entirely consistent, that women in all of the ethnic groups succeed more than men in satisfying this need through contact with the nurse. The evidence does not indicate, however, that less educated, that is, lower-class, clients are distinguished by an especially high level in satisfaction of this need through the nurse.

CATHARSIS HYPOTHESIS

Table 7 shows that the catharsis hypothesis is confirmed with respect to the Kupat Holim physician: members of Kupat Holim with a high need for catharsis and a tendency to define themselves as ill report more success than other Kupat Holim members in obtaining satisfaction of this need from the clinic doctor. The difference is significant but not very large.

The hypothesis is not confirmed, however, for the Kupat Holim nurse. Although clients with a high tendency to define themselves as ill are more successful than those with a low tendency in obtaining satisfaction of the catharsis need from the Kupat Holim nurse, this occurs regardless of the level of their own need and therefore does not confirm our prediction.

A more detailed look at the data shows that none of the subgroups of the population—broken into ethnic, residence, age, sex, and education categories—reveals complete confirmation of the catharsis hypothesis with respect to the clinic physician. However, we do find partial confirmation among the Kurdish members of Kupat Holim: Kurds characterized by a high need for catharsis report comparatively frequent satisfaction of this need from the Kupat Holim physician. This trend emerges fairly consistently in most subgroups of the Kurdish population. While it cannot be argued that this represents a complete confirmation of the hypothesis, it does provide supportive data. It will be recalled (see Chapter One) that the tendency to define oneself as ill was introduced as a filter mechanism in an effort to sift out those members of Kupat Holim who might be likely to seek alternative loci in the social system to satisfy their need. The present findings suggest that the Kupat Holim physician does provide a source of satisfaction for

Table 6

Perception of Doctor and Nurse as Satisfying Catharsis Need by Ethnic Groups

Percentage of Clients who perceive Kupat Holim doctor as:

	Sympathetic, understanding, and supportive	Occasionally supportive and occasionally nonsupportive	Unsympathetic, un-understanding, and nonsupportive	N
Moroccans	26	61	13	576
Kurds	20	64	16	493
Rumanians	19	59	22[a]	531
Poles	19	68	13	220

Percentage of Clients who perceive Kupat Holim nurse as:

	Sympathetic, understanding, and supportive	Occasionally supportive and occasionally nonsupportive	Unsympathetic, un-understanding, and nonsupportive	N
Moroccans	18[b]	68	14	572
Kurds	17	70	13	495
Rumanians	13	73	14	528
Poles	11	76	13	220

[a] The difference between the Rumanians and all of the other groups combined is significant. $X^2 = 18.39$, D.F. $= 2$, P $< .001$.

[b] The difference between the non-Europeans (combined Moroccans and Kurds) and the Europeans (combined Rumanians and Poles) is significant. $X^2 = 7.18$, D.F. $= 2$, $.05 > P > .02$.

Table 7

PHYSICIANS' SATISFACTION OF CATHARSIS NEED AS REPORTED BY "NEED-TENDENCY" GROUPS

Percentage of Clients who perceive Kupat Holim doctor as:

Need for Catharsis, Tendency to Define Oneself as Ill	Sympathetic, understanding, and supportive	Occasionally supportive and occasionally nonsupportive	Unsympathetic, un-understanding, and nonsupportive	N
High need, high tendency	26[a]	57	17	338
High need, low tendency	19	61	20	309
Low need, high tendency	22	65	13	661
Low need, low tendency	19	63	18	514

[a] The difference between this critical group and all three others is significant. $X^2 = 7.19$, D.F. $= 2$, $.05 > P > .02$.

the catharsis need among Kurdish immigrants: when a high need exists they succeed in satisfying it within the Kupat Holim context through the clinic physician. If other alternatives do not exist, the tendency variable does not play the expected filtering role.

A similar pattern is shown by Kurdish respondents with respect to the Kupat Holim nurse: those with a high need for catharsis tend more frequently to report success in satisfying that need through her. Here again the tendency variable does not discriminate as predicted. While the findings are less consistent than those reported with respect to the physician, they do suggest that Kurdish respondents with a comparatively high need for catharsis tend to satisfy that need through the Kupat Holim clinic—in their contacts both with the physician and with the nurse.

The urban Rumanians are the only group in our population to show complete confirmation of the catharsis hypothesis with the Kupat Holim nurse. All subgroups among them reveal a consistent confirming picture: both sexes, all age groups, and all levels of education. There is therefore no basis to suppose that the nurse is especially congenial to one particular stratum of the urban Rumanian population, for example, the less educated or the females. This picture suggests that the urban Rumanians are in fact seeking out this latent function with the nurse along the lines we have proposed.

NEED SATISFACTION

Tables 8 and 9 divide the need-tendency typology in terms of respondents' feeling that the need for catharsis is satisfied or not by the physician or the nurse. We then observe reported patterns of utilization and satisfaction with Kupat Holim services in these subgroups.

Focusing first on reported frequency of clinic utilization (sections A of Tables 8 and 9), we see a similar patterning with respect to clinic utilization to both the doctor and the nurse: the subgroups characterized by a high need for catharsis and a high tendency to define themselves as ill are high utilizers. What is remarkable about this picture is the fact that high utilization occurs in the critical group *whether or not* the need for catharsis has been satisfied by the Kupat Holim personnel. While the data in both

Table 8

UTILIZATION AND ATTITUDE PATTERNS TOWARD KUPAT HOLIM: CATHARSIS NEED SATISFACTION THROUGH PHYSICIAN

Need for Catharsis, Tendency to Define Oneself as Ill	A Percentage who report 20 or more visits a year to Kupat Holim doctor		B Percentage who report themselves satisfied with medical care of Kupat Holim[a]		C Percentage who use only Kupat Holim; do not use private or other clinics	
	Perceive Kupat Holim doctor as:[b]		Perceive Kupat Holim doctor as:		Perceive Kupat Holim doctor as:	
	Generally sympathetic, understanding, and supportive	Generally unsympathetic, un-understanding and nonsupportive	Generally sympathetic, understanding, and supportive	Generally unsympathetic, un-understanding, and nonsupportive	Generally sympathetic, understanding, and supportive	Generally unsympathetic, un-understanding, and nonsupportive
High need, high tendency ..	30 (181)	26 (143)	74 (186)	46 (147)	82 (175)	73 (145)
High need, low tendency ...	11 (140)	10 (158)	63 (144)	51 (156)	74 (140)	67 (153)
Low need, high tendency ...	19 (361)	18 (282)	78 (368)	58 (283)	86 (363)	78 (282)
Low need, low tendency	9 (231)	8 (273)	76 (229)	59 (269)	78 (226)	76 (275)

[a] Based on a Guttman scale defined by the following items: Is it generally easy or difficult to get to see a Kupat Holim doctor? Are you satisfied with the personal attitude of Kupat Holim doctors to you? Do you believe that you get really good medical care from Kupat Holim doctors? Each item was dichotomized. R = .85.

[b] In order to assure a sufficient number of cases, the scale defining reported satisfaction of catharsis need by the physician was dichotomized and not trichotomized as in Table 7.

Table 9

UTILIZATION AND ATTITUDE PATTERNS TOWARD KUPAT HOLIM: CATHARSIS NEED SATISFACTION THROUGH NURSE

Need for Catharsis, Tendency to Define Oneself as Ill	A — Percentage who report 20 or more visits a year to Kupat Holim nurse:[b]		B — Percentage who report themselves satisfied with medical care of Kupat Holim[a]		C — Percentage who use only Kupat Holim; do not use private or other clinics	
	Perceive Kupat Holim nurse as:[b]		*Perceive Kupat Holim nurse as:*		*Perceive Kupat Holim nurse as:*	
	Generally sympathetic, understanding, and supportive	*Generally unsympathetic, un-understanding, and nonsupportive*	*Generally sympathetic, understanding, and supportive*	*Generally unsympathetic, un-understanding, and nonsupportive*	*Generally sympathetic, understanding, and supportive*	*Generally unsympathetic, un-understanding, and nonsupportive*
High need, high tendency ..	27 (130)	24 (190)	58 (139)	64 (194)	76 (133)	80 (187)
High need, low tendency ...	15 (96)	8 (198)	61 (98)	55 (201)	75 (93)	69 (200)
Low need, high tendency ...	19 (258)	16 (361)	77 (277)	64 (272)	83 (278)	82 (365)
Low need, low tendency	16 (133)	5 (353)	77 (142)	62 (354)	77 (141)	77 (355)

[a] See footnote a, Table 8.

[b] In order to assure a sufficient number of cases, the scale defining reported satisfaction of catharsis need by the nurse was dichotomized and not trichotomized as in Table 7.

tables indicate that a high tendency to define oneself as ill increases the frequency of utilization, it is clear that the specific combination of need for catharsis and the tendency increases it even more. In view of their importance to our hypothesis we have checked these findings among respondents who report themselves to be generally sick or generally healthy and the picture we have described is confirmed in three of the four comparisons. The exception is the healthy respondents among whom the critical group does not report higher doctor attendance than the remainder of the population. At the same time it is not markedly low in frequency of doctor utilization.

These findings are in line with our hypothesis and suggest that clients are seeking out the latent function of the institution that will satisfy this particular need. The fact that this comparatively high utilization occurs whether or not the need is reportedly satisfied suggests that we may be witnessing both a rational enjoyment of the latent function and a ritual pattern of attendance. The former occurs among those who report high satisfaction of the need for catharsis; the latter occurs when the need is not markedly satisfied but clients attend the clinic with high frequency apparently in the expectation of activating the latent function. The ritual pattern, while possibly associated with a certain measure of frustration, is based on clients' belief and expectation that the clinic physician and nurse should and probably will at some time fulfill the need for catharsis. Such a pattern presumably could persist for a prolonged period until extinguished by consistent frustration.

Examining section B of Tables 8 and 9 concerning the level of satisfaction with Kupat Holim services, we do not find especially high satisfaction among those with a high need for catharsis and a high tendency who report satisfaction of this need (the upper left-hand group). In general these tables indicate that satisfaction of the need for catharsis, particularly by the clinic physician, tends to increase overall satisfaction with clinic services. But this does not occur with more marked frequency in the critical subgroup. Neither do we find that clients in the critical group who succeed in satisfying the need show more frequent exclusive use of Kupat Holim to the exclusion of private or other medical services (Section C of Tables 8 and 9).

Thus our general conclusions concerning the consequences of need satisfaction refer mostly to the frequency of utilization of clinic facilities. The findings point to the irrelevance of satisfaction of the catharsis need in conditioning utilization, but indicate that the need-tendency typology is an efficient predictor of high clinic usage: clients characterized by a high need for catharsis and a high tendency to define themselves as ill appear to be the most frequent attenders both to the clinic doctor and nurse.

PHYSICIANS' RESPONSE

We have noted that physicians may differ in their own professional role definitions: they may view satisfaction of the need for catharsis as an integral part of their diagnostic and therapeutic functions—or they may feel that satisfaction of this need falls more appropriately in the realm of the psychiatrist or social worker. Furthermore, with the best intentions in the world, many doctors may feel so hampered by the medical bureaucratic structure and by the pressures of clients and time, as to be unable to satisfy this need despite their desire to do so.

Physicians' response to the need for catharsis was measured in terms of three questions. The doctors were first presented with the following statement:

Some Rumanian (or Moroccan) patients like the doctor to sit and listen to them as they talk and pour their hearts out about all sorts of problems relating both to their health and to other subjects.

Under ordinary working conditions in your clinic, how do you respond to such patients?

a. When they talk about purely medical problems:
   1. I encourage them to talk.
   2. I permit them to talk.
   3. I try to limit them to the essentials of the medical problem.

b. When they talk about problems which are only indirectly related to their health:
   1. I encourage them to talk.
   2. I permit them to talk.
   3. I try to limit them.

    4. I limit them exclusively to subjects directly connected to the medical problem.

c. When they talk about subjects which may not be related to the medical problem at all:

    1. I encourage them to talk.

    2. I permit them to talk.

    3. I try to limit them.

    4. I limit them to subjects which deal only with the medical problem.

These questions defined a Guttman scale. Dichotomizing the three items yielded four scale types. For physicians reporting on Moroccan patients, $R = .96$. For physicians reporting on Rumanian patients $R = .94$. The items were dichotomized as follows: Question a. categories 1, 2 = gives catharsis; category 3 = does not give catharsis; Question b. categories 1, 2 = gives catharsis; categories 3, 4 = does not give catharsis; Question c. categories 1, 2 = gives catharsis; categories 3, 4 = does not give catharsis. The scale continuum was dichotomized with two scale types defined as those doctors who give more catharsis and two scale types defined as those who give less or none.

About two-thirds of the physicians report that they provide satisfaction for the catharsis needs of patients but there is no difference in physicians' reported response to the two ethnic groups of patients. It will be recalled that this picture is contrary to our expectation that there would be greater responsiveness to Rumanian than to Moroccan patients.

Of all the needs discussed, satisfaction of the catharsis need comes closest to a medical norm. Indeed, many physicians define it as part of their legitimate professional obligation. While some may feel that fulfillment of this need falls more within the realm of other professionals (the psychiatrist, the religious leader, the public health nurse, or the social worker), few would deny that the general practitioner should fulfill this need on some level. Even those who would limit most extremely the satisfaction of this need would recognize that some relevant diagnostic information concerning the patient's health could emerge when the patient unburdens himself.

The close relationship of this function to the diagnostic

and possibly to the curative role of the physician helps explain the
similarity in physicians' response to the two ethnic groups (Moroccans and Rumanians). Medical norms press strongly toward equal
treatment for all and do not condone differential orientations to
clients in terms of their ethnic origin. This contrasts with the latent
function of giving status (see Chapter Nine), for example, which
is marginal to the actual diagnostic or curative process and conse-
quently is more open to the impingement of nonmedical norms.
We may assume that physicians' responses in the present case were
conditioned by norms of their professional role.

It will be recalled that we are basing this discussion on
physicians' reports of their behavior in a clinic situation and not on
actual observations of such behavior. To the extent that distortion
is occurring, one might expect it to appear when more strictly medical behavior is being described. Our data do not permit us to estimate the extent of possible distortion and our conclusion can only
refer to the empirical findings which indicate absence of differences
in physicians' response to the catharsis needs of the two ethnic
groups of patients.

In the course of the discussions, physicians referred repeatedly to patients' need to talk and unburden themselves in the
clinic: "Patients should be able to come and talk to get some encouragement from us. We can't throw them out. They have all sorts
of problems." "They want special attention and need someone to
listen to them. That's why they come to the doctor for every little
thing—even a temperature of 37.2." "Mothers love to come and tell
me over and over again about their children . . . and not always
about their health."

Many doctors show a certain awareness that provision of a setting for catharsis falls appropriately within their professional role area.
They feel that doctors should respond to this need: "I sit and listen to
them talk five or even ten minutes—as long as they like. The others
outside in the waiting room can wait. I know that this is the right way
to practice medicine." "The art of medicine requires understanding
and communication. Sometimes a patient needs encouragement to
go back to work and sometimes he should be encouraged to rest."
"I feel that we fill an important role: we are like priests. People
come and talk with us. Take a woman who has had an argument

with her husband. The first place she turns is to the Kupat Holim clinic doctor. I'm not at all sure she is justified in coming from a medical point of view, but we can't help but receive her." "Often the doctor is the only person willing to listen to the patient talk. When a mother of ten children comes here to pour out her heart, she usually has no one at home who will listen to her. And the doctor should understand this and give her a chance to talk."

There is also some mention of the pressures of practice that sometimes prevent the doctor from carrying out his professional role: "With good will we can always communicate with patients even without knowing their language. Except that sometimes time is so limited and the pressure in the waiting room is so great that this is very difficult."

SUMMARY

The need for catharsis is fairly equally distributed among the ethnic groups we have observed. This finding is all the more remarkable when we consider the extreme differences in background and culture among them and it provides some basis to believe that the impact of the acculturation and adjustment process is similar in many respects for these ethnic groups.

Clients' perception of the Kupat Holim physician's willingness to listen sympathetically and supportively also shows few differences among the ethnic groups. Only the urban Rumanians, and particularly the younger members of this group, show a somewhat greater dissatisfaction with the physician in this regard.

We proposed that some measure of the catharsis-satisfying role of the physician might rub off onto the Kupat Holim nurse—particularly for clients who would feel themselves closer to her from the point of view of social status. And in fact the evidence does indicate that the two non-European groups—the Moroccans and the Kurds—express somewhat greater satisfaction than the Europeans with the nurse as a sympathetic, supportive listener. The same is true of the women in the population. Such findings confirm Simmons' impression and suggest that people whose status or role is closer to that of the nurse may succeed in satisfying their need for catharsis through her (Simmons, 1958a; 1958b).

At the same time it does not appear that the nurse has taken over the catharsis-satisfying role of the physician entirely. On the whole, doctors are described as performing this role more frequently than nurses. In a general sense we may therefore conclude that both members of the clinic team perform this role: the physician does so more frequently but the nurse succeeds somewhat more in satisfying this need among clients of a specific sort, that is, non-Europeans and women.

When we look at physicians' reports of their own clinic behavior, we find two-thirds of them stating that they permit clients to talk and unburden themselves freely even on subjects which might be medically irrelevant. The remaining one-third state that they impose some limits on clients' freedom to talk. Furthermore, physicians report that they are equally permissive in this regard to European and non-European patients, that is, Rumanians and Moroccans. We have suggested that catharsis-giving is probably included by many physicians among the manifest functions of the professional role. If this is the case, we would expect universalistic medical norms to condition this behavior so that professional orientations to different ethnic groups would tend to be more or less similar. Of course we are basing our conclusion on reported behavior by physicians rather than on clinic observations and are therefore unable to estimate possible distortions in such reports.

What conclusions can be drawn about the specific hypothesis concerning satisfaction of the need for catharsis by Kupat Holim personnel? Is there an empirical basis for the theory that this represents a latent function of the medical institution which may attract clients to utilize the institution?

The answer to this question is affirmative. Our data point to a general confirmation of the prediction that the need-tendency group will report satisfaction of its need for catharsis through the Kupat Holim physician. This does not occur in response to questions concerning the Kupat Holim nurse. What is more, the same group shows a significantly higher attendance to see both the doctor and the nurse. It is of considerable interest that this comparatively high attendance occurs whether or not clients report satisfaction of their need. We have suggested that this pattern may represent both an enjoyment of the latent function (among those who report satisfaction of the need) and a ritual type of attendance (among those who do not report need satisfaction).

Two of the ethnic groups under observation show unique patterns of perception and behavior in this area: the Kurds and the urban Rumanians.

The Kurds, who are the least Western of the ethnic groups included in the study, suggest a confirmation of the hypothesis but not entirely in terms of our specific formulation. Kurds with a comparatively high need for catharsis report a large measure of satisfaction of that need through their contacts with the Kupat Holim physician and nurse. However, while the need plays the predicted role, the tendency—which was hypothesized to discriminate between those who would seek satisfaction in the Kupat Holim context and those who would seek alternative loci for need satisfaction—does not play such a role. Furthermore, the Kurds report a high frequency of clinic attendance to see both the doctor and the nurse.

The combination of these findings yields a picture in which the Kurds emerge as most clearly supporting the hypothesis on both a behavioral (that is, utilization) and a perception level. If we look at the critical group, that is, the subgroup with both a high need for catharsis and a tendency to define themselves as ill, we find that it is distinguished both by a comparatively high frequency of reported utilization of clinic facilities and by a high level of satisfaction of the need for catharsis through contact with the physician and the nurse.

It is certainly of some interest that the clearest activation of the latent function occurs in the most traditional of the ethnic groups observed. This is not because the need for catharsis is greater among the Kurds: the level of need does not differ substantially among the four ethnic groups. It is nevertheless worth considering the possibility that a more refined measure might show that the most traditional group feels the absence of a supportive extended family system more acutely so that a greater pressure is set up to seek available loci to satisfy it. This leads them to the Kupat Holim personnel.

The urban Rumanians also show a unique and interesting pattern. The data indicate that this group confirms the hypothesis on a behavioral level for both physician and nurse, that is, utilization, and on a perception level for the nurse. This is to say that urban Rumanians characterized by a high need for catharsis and a high tendency to define themselves as ill report comparatively high satisfaction of that need through the Kupat Holim nurse but attend the clinic with comparatively high frequency to see both the doctor and the nurse. At the same time it is worth recalling that the urban Rumanians express somewhat greater dissatisfaction than the other ethnic groups with the Kupat Holim physician as a sympathetic, supportive listener. The picture that emerges is therefore structured differently for the Kupat Holim physician and nurse.

We may term the pattern associated with the Kupat Holim physician as ritualistic: the subgroup with a high need and tendency does not report especially high satisfaction of the need but does attend the clinic comparatively frequently to see the doctor. The ritualism expresses itself in the fact that behavior occurs even though satisfaction is not especially marked.

With respect to the Kupat Holim nurse, behavior may be considered more rational: the urban Rumanians appear to be taking advantage of the latent function. This conclusion is based on the fact that the subgroup with a high need and tendency not only reports itself markedly satisfied with the nurse but also attends the clinic with comparatively high frequency in order to see her. In this context it is worth recalling the relative dissatisfaction expressed by urban Rumanians with respect to the willingness of the Kupat Holim physician to listen to them sympathetically and supportively. It would therefore appear that urban Rumanians are using the nurse to obtain satisfaction of their need for catharsis, possibly as a result of failing to satisfy this need with the clinic physician. It is difficult to determine just why this pattern should occur specifically among the urban Rumanian clients, unless it is a function of a unique local situation in the Kupat Holim clinic.

The remaining ethnic groups are not distinguished by clearly defined patterns.

7

Coping with Failure

Illness represents one way of coping with failure in Western society. To be sick means to be unable to fulfill tasks; it is an acceptable avoidance of responsibilities. Sensing failure, one can justify this failure, to oneself or to significant reference groups, in terms of one's inability to perform as a result of illness. Parsons' (1951) analysis suggests that people who feel failure, for whatever reason, may seek out the sick role in order to legitimize their failure to perform adequately. Balint (1966; also Stoekle et al., 1964) has also noted that "people who for some reason find it difficult to cope with the problems of life, resort to becoming ill." At the same time it is worth noting that Parsons has not considered the fact that in an activity-oriented culture, illness may also be so guilt-producing that people may seek to escape from or avoid the role.

In addition to providing a rationale for failure, illness can contribute to an individual's efforts to cope with failure in other ways. When the failure involves an inability to care for or maintain oneself, illness may justify other people's assuming the care-taking function. This is accomplished either through other individuals stepping in or through hospitalization or institutionalization. Failure to obtain certain desired goals can also be coped with through illness. This is especially relevant in a social system which uses illness as a criterion for the distribution of certain scarce rewards, such as better housing, easier work, social welfare benefits, tax benefits, change of residence, and many others. When such rewards are in scarce supply in the society, some mechanism must be devised to determine the basis of their allocation. In Israel illness is sometimes utilized as such an allocative tool. This means that people who fail to obtain these goals through their own efforts can cope with that failure by gaining at least some of them through illness (Moses and Hoek, 1961).

Feelings of failure represent a subjective state that can arise from different situations. Inadequate role performance as measured by one's own expectations or against the performance of others can bring about this feeling. Immigrants are especially vulnerable to such feelings of failure because they are often impressed into roles for which they have been inadequately prepared. In addition they may be frustrated by the realities of what may have been for them the "Promised Land" and may tend to selective recall of a rosy past in the old country. In addition, immigrants' feelings that opportunities or channels of social mobility are not always accessible to them on an equal basis could induce a feeling of failure among them. Such unequal access may be real or only perceived but its implications for feelings of failure remain. All of these considerations lead us to believe that immigrants are particularly prone to utilize illness in their efforts to cope with failure. Berle (1958) has noted several of the above patterns among Puerto Rican immigrants in New York and has pointed explicitly to the connection between feelings of failure and illness.

In Western society, illness cannot be self-defined, but must be authorized by an acceptable professional, namely the physician. He carries the unique authority to legitimize illness. From this point of view the medical institution, with the physician as its central figure, plays a major role in contributing to patients' efforts to cope with failure.

In fact, legitimation of illness is a manifest function of the medical institution. The latent function of such legitimation relates to its consequences for patients' coping with failure. By legitimizing illness, the physician enables the patient to utilize one of the mechanisms described above for coping with failure. Such a situation suggests that people who feel failure will be highly motivated to seek out the sick role and will desire legitimation for that role from the physician.

Proper functioning of the medical institution requires that legitimation is requested and given only when a "real" case of illness is being considered. The physician is often under some pressure to identify the "real" cases, especially when borderlines are ambiguous and the possibility of error can be a source of some anxiety to him. However, it is clear from Field's (1957) research and from observation of the Kupat Holim clinics that this function is, by its nature, subject to distortion, especially by malingerers. It would appear that requests for formal legitimation of illness may run fairly high in Kupat Holim. Morag (1966) estimates on the basis of systematic observations in Kupat Holim clinics that 11 per cent of all requests made by patients are for legitimation in the form of a *petek*, a formal certification attesting to the client's illness. In Britain, the frequency of such requests is estimated to run between 14 per cent and 25 per cent (Fry, 1952; Backett, Heady, and Evans, 1954).

Of course it is difficult to judge whether such frequencies of requests are really high. In Israel the need for formal legitimation of illness is at least partly imposed by the social system, which frequently requires such legitimation as a prerequisite for many benefits and rewards. Even when an individual does not need to be ill in order to cope with failure, he may require a *petek* in order to obtain better housing, easier work, or social welfare benefits (Moses and Hoek, 1961). Those segments of the population which are better able to obtain scarce rewards on the basis of their own efforts and are therefore less dependent on public institutions would probably require such certifications less frequently. When housing can be obtained more or less by one's own efforts, when one has skills which are negotiable in the job market, or if one is not in need of welfare benefits, the objective need for a formal legitimation of illness is probably lower. Furthermore, some people may be more skilled and experienced at maneuvering through much of the red tape of the nonmedical bureaucracies; they may be able to obtain the sought-after privileges without producing a medical legitimation.

Physicians may react with some disfavor to subgroups of patients who are perceived as exerting more than their share of demands for legitimation of illness. Malingering and using the physician to obtain nontherapeutic goals represent deviant forms of the patient role and as such will evoke a negative response by doctors who resent being exploited. This annoyance on the part of the physician is reinforced by the ambiguity of many symptoms and the consequent difficulty of defining malingerers. We have already noted the strain inherent in such a situation and the pressure it places on the physician. All of these factors combine to make the physician impatient and possibly hostile to patients who are perceived as exerting undue demand for the *petek*.

There is a certain circularity in the patterns of perception and response within the social system made up of the doctor and his patient. The patient may respond to the physician's annoyance or impatience by deviating further from the expected patient role; additional deviance reinforces the doctor's resentment. And so on. Furthermore, the logic of the argument proposed in this monograph is that failure of the physician to satisfy patients' needs—which are not only of a strictly medical nature—may intensify the patient's desire to obtain such satisfaction. Prolonged frustration may lead him to seek satisfaction elsewhere, but probably only after a period of learning. What is more, the need for legitimation of illness cannot in fact be satisfied in other than medical institutional contexts. The only alternative to the specific Kupat Holim context would be another medical institution or private doctor, and for lower income groups, these alternatives may not be practicable. The pressures to obtain satisfaction for this particular need within the Kupat Holim context are therefore especially strong.

OVERVIEW OF VARIABLES

Feeling of failure was examined in four areas of the respondent's life: major role area (for men: providing for the family's livelihood; for women: running the household), relationships with children, relationships with spouse, and relationships with members of the extended family. Respondents who were not married, did not have children, or did not have family were excluded from this analysis. There were a total of 382 respondents excluded on this basis. Feeling of failure refers to statements by respondents that they feel failure in two or more of the four areas considered. (The four items were tested for scalability and no order was found among them. We have therefore followed the procedure of simply counting the number of areas in which feeling of failure is reported, without regard to order.)

The differences among the four ethnic groups in feeling failure are small. Roughly half of each group report feeling failure in two or more of the four areas. We have noted that such feelings are subjective and are not necessarily positively correlated with objective measures of success or failure. If we observe feeling of failure in three or four areas, we find the Rumanians to be somewhat lower than the other groups.

Checking the feeling of failure among subgroups of the population shows men to express such feeling more frequently than women. Among the Moroccan and Kurdish groups we also find that feelings of failure are more widespread in urban than in rural communities.

The problem of measuring success in obtaining legitimation of illness proved to be a thorny one. The physician's very recognition and acceptance of the individual as sick permits the patient to enter the sick role and in this manner to gain the desired legitimation. It will be recalled that our research procedure involved an examination of attitudes and orientations of members of Kupat Holim and of a group of clinic physicians but did not include direct observations in the clinic situation. We were therefore unable to determine directly when physicians do or do not give legitimation for illness.

The logic of our theoretical model leads to the following implicit question: "Does the physician accept and define you as ill when you want him to?" Because such a question could not be asked directly, another approach was sought. People who feel failure will believe that provision of help in coping with this failure is a central and crucial function of the Kupat Holim clinic. More than others, they will feel that the granting of the *petek,* the formal certification of illness, is an important aspect of clinic activities. This is because need for a goal heightens perception of the salience of the means to that goal, especially in an institutional context which exercises exclusive control over those means. In the present case the *petek* represents the formal means to the goal.

We would further expect that people characterized by a feeling of failure as well as a tendency to define themselves as ill would be high clinic utilizers. Clinic attendance can be thought of as a direct means for obtaining legitimation for illness. In contrast to the other hypotheses, in this case we may consider the frequency of clinic attendance as a direct dependent variable in testing the hypothesis concerning coping with failure. This is the case because coming to the clinic by definition implies a desire to enter the sick role and to obtain legitimation for illness.

Table 10 shows the importance attributed to *petek*-granting by the ethnic groups; it shows that the Moroccans and Kurds perceive this function as more central and crucial to Kupat Holim than do the European groups. This despite the fact, already noted, that the non-Europeans as a whole do not express a greater feeling of failure. Analysis by ethnic, sex, age, and education groups shows no clearly patterned differences among these subgroups. The non-medical bureaucratic system with its demands for formal certification of illness in exchange for certain types of rewards may be exerting differential pressure on the ethnic groups and the non-Europeans might tend to be more subject to it. On the other hand, it is also possible that this image of the clinic is more prevalent in the subculture of the non-European groups.

TESTING THE HYPOTHESIS

As noted, we will test the hypothesis relating to coping with failure on two dependent variables: the first concerns respondents' perception of the importance and centrality of *petek*-granting in Kupat Holim, while the second refers to the frequency of Kupat Holim attendance.

Table 11 indicates that the hypothesis is confirmed on both of these dependent variables. In both cases the critical group is significantly different from the other three combined. However, a more detailed analysis of subgroups of the population shows this

Table 10

Importance Attributed to the *Petek* and Frequency of Clinic Attendance

	Percentage who believe that petek-granting is:			Percentage reporting 20 or more visits a year to Kupat Holim doctor	N
	Very Important[a]	*Somewhat Important*	*Not Very Important*		
Moroccans	39	42	19	13	586
Kurds	38	42	20	24	506
Rumanians	17	40	43	14	539
Poles	21	42	37	5	229

[a] The difference between the non-Europeans (combined Moroccans and Kurds) and Europeans (combined Rumanians and Poles) is significant: $X^2 = 132.44$; D.F. $= 2$; P $< .001$.

Table 11

IMPORTANCE ATTRIBUTED TO THE Petek AMONG "NEED-TENDENCY" TYPES

Feeling of Failure, Tendency to Define Oneself as Ill	Percentage of clients who believe that petek-granting is:			Percentage of clients reporting 20 or more visits a year to Kupat Holim doctor	N
	Very important	Somewhat important	Not Very important		
Feel failure, high tendency	39[a]	43	18	28[b]	354
Feel failure, low tendency	25	48	27	12	337
Do not feel failure, high tendency	35	40	25	15	469
Do not feel failure, low tendency	26	36	38	7	348

[a] The difference between the critical group and the three other groups combined is significant. $X^2 = 33.97$, D.F. = 2, P < .001.

[b] The difference between the critical group and the other three groups combined is significant. $X^2 = 51.99$, D.F. = 1, P < .001.

conclusion to be only partially substantiated. When we look separately at the ethnic groups, we find that only the rural Moroccans
confirm the hypothesis on the first dependent variable, perception
of certification as a central function of Kupat Holim. All observed
subgroups among the rural Moroccans show the same consistent
confirming pattern. But this does not occur in the remaining ethnic
groups. On the other hand, we find that practically all of the
ethnic-residential groups confirm the hypothesis with respect to the
utilization variable. Our general conclusion must therefore be that
people characterized by a feeling of failure and a tendency to define
themselves as ill are generally high frequency utilizers of the physicians' services, but the majority of them do not differ from the remainder of the population in believing that certification of illness
is a central function of Kupat Holim.

To determine whether frequency of clinic attendance could
be distorted by actual illness, the population was further divided
into self-defined sick and healthy subgroups and the hypothesis
tested again with frequency of attendance as the dependent variable.
The findings noted in Table 11 were completely confirmed. What is
most remarkable, and perhaps an indication of the strength of our
prediction, is the fact that 24 per cent of the self-defined healthy
members of Kupat Holim in the critical group report visiting their
physician more than ten times during the past year. Surely this is
an extraordinarily high frequency of clinic attendance for healthy
people.

PHYSICIANS' RESPONSE

The nature of our observations does not permit us to determine directly whether and how often physicians provide for legitimation of illness. The approach taken here has been to focus on
attitudes and feelings concerning requests for certification and reported styles of response. The first question raised concerns physicians' perception of differential demands by ethnic groups for
formal certification of illness. We have already noted that doctors
may resent patients who are thought to be exerting more than their
share of demands for legitimation of illness. Fearing exploitation
by malingerers, physicians might be likely to respond with exaggerated skepticism and severity to members of ethnic groups thought

to be chronic malingerers and therefore seekers of the *petek*. Stereo-typed patterns of perception could well distort their orientation to such patients and could even result in failure to grant certification when in fact an unbiased medical approach would find it justified.

The empirical procedure was to tap two dimensions of this problem: the first concerned physicians' perception of the comparative frequency of requests for legitimation by the ethnic groups, while the second attempted to focus on reported style of response to patients' demands for legitimation.

Physicians were first presented with the following statement:

Some doctors believe that immigrants from Morocco (or Rumania) often become ill because sickness provides a way to justify some sort of failure in their everyday life.

Two types of questions were then posed:

Does the doctor perceive this phenomenon to be widespread among Moroccan (or Rumanian) patients?

a. From your experience would you say that this cause of illness is particularly widespread among Moroccan (or Rumanian) immigrants?

   1. Extremely widespread.
   2. Somewhat widespread.
   3. Not particularly widespread.
   4. Rare.

The second type of questions concerned the doctor's response to patients of this sort: with understanding and support, or unsympathetically and critically.

b. How do you generally behave toward such Moroccan (or Rumanian) patients?

   1. With sympathy and understanding.
   2. They annoy me but I try not to show it.
   3. They annoy me, and I think the patient should know it.

c. When you encounter a Moroccan (or Rumanian) patient of this sort, how do you treat him?

   1. I treat him strictly from a medical point of view.
   2. I treat him medically, but try to persuade him to carry out his responsibilities at work or in his family.
   3. I treat him medically, but definitely do not permit him to exploit illness to justify failure.

    d. What in your opinion is the best approach to such patients?

        1. They should be treated only from a medical point of view.

        2. They should be treated medically, but an attempt should be made to persuade them to fulfill their responsibilities at work or in their family.

        3. They should be treated medically but under no circumstances should be helped to justify their failure.

Table 12 shows that Moroccans are more frequently perceived by physicians to be sick as a result of a feeling of failure: 60 per cent of the doctors in the study reported this phenomenon to be somewhat or extremely widespread among Moroccan patients while only 17 per cent perceive this to be the case among Rumanians (question a). Furthermore, when asked how they generally respond, physicians report giving relatively more sympathy and understanding to Rumanian than to Moroccan patients (question b).

A more detailed analysis which breaks the physicians into subgroups by age, length of time in the country, and seniority in the profession shows that younger physicians as well as those who have arrived more recently in the country and are newer in the profession tend to give both Moroccans and Rumanians somewhat less sympathy and understanding. We are unable to determine from these data whether age, greater seniority, and experience of practice in Israel tend to increase physicians' sympathy and understanding of patients or whether we may be dealing with different types of doctors, characterized by varying professional orientations. In any case this tendency does not change the finding reported from Table 12, namely that all subgroups of physicians report dispensing more sympathy and understanding to Rumanian than to Moroccan patients.

Subgroups of physicians do not differ significantly on the other three questions used to tap response to the need for legitimation of failure.

When asked about the quality of medical care given, physicians show no differences in their orientation to the two ethnic groups (Table 12, questions c and d). We have already noted that in matters having a manifest implication for medical treatment physicians fail to show differences on our instrument in their orienta-

Table 12

Physicians' Response to Need for Coping with Failure

Patient Group	Percentage of physicians who perceive illness caused by failure to be widespread[a]	Percentage of physicians who support patients who are sick as a result of failure			N
		Sympathetic and understanding[b]	Gives noncritical, strictly medical treatment[c]	Believes in noncritical, strictly medical treatment[d]	
Rumanians	17	59	11	8	230
Moroccans	60	48	10	7	113

[a] Categories 1 and 2 of question a.
[b] Category 1 of question b.
[c] Category 1 of question c. We assume here that "strictly medical treatment" represents a noncritical and relatively supportive attitude by the physician in this context. This assumption is made in terms of the other categories of response, which imply criticism, for example, "persuading him to fulfill his obligations," "preventing him from exploiting illness."
[d] Category 1 in question d. "Strictly medical treatment" represents a supportive attitude by the physician in this context.

tion to different ethnic groups of patients. This was true with respect
to physicians' reports of their satisfaction of patients' need for
catharsis (Chapter Six) and it appears to be true in those questions
discussed here which refer explicitly to the quality of medical care
given. We have suggested that the universalistic norm of the medical profession may be exerting more of an influence when physicians
are called upon to answer this type of question than when the questions are of a more general nature and do not make overt reference
to the specific nature of the medical care dispensed.

Nevertheless it seems reasonable to wonder whether the
quality of medical care is not affected by differential patterns of
perception and reported response to the ethnic groups. Can the
physician behave in the same way to the Moroccan and to the
Rumanian patient when he "knows" that the Moroccan is more
likely to be coming to the clinic for reasons having to do with failure rather than for strictly medical problems? Our guess is that this
is probably very difficult for most doctors.

In their discussions doctors repeatedly referred to patients'
requests for certificates as a chronic problem: "Every little thing
requires a certificate. A person wants to buy a refrigerator—a
certificate; to move to a new apartment—a certificate; an easier
job—a certificate. All we do is write and write certificates. There's
no end to it."

Despite some exaggeration by this doctor it is clear that this
general feeling is widespread among the physicians. Not only does
certificate writing take valuable time away from the clinical aspects
of practice, but it seems to leave the physician with an uncom-
fortable feeling of possible exploitation by patients: "When a patient comes in complaining of headaches and all sorts of other pains,
I always wonder if he really wants some sick leave or if he needs a
certificate to get out of work."

Many doctors seem aware of the relationship of their own
role as certificate-givers and the larger institutional structure which
imposes this role on them. One reason the demand for certificates
is so high is that other organizations and public bodies require
people to produce them: "The Social Welfare offices and the immigration authorities all send people to us for certificates." "People
are sent to me from the National Insurance offices; Kupat Holim

merely serves as an agent for the other bodies." "We provide sickness certificates for employers, for schools, and for the police. We even do it for the army." "Anyone who wants to get anything in Israel does it through a medical certificate. Without one he can't get an interview for a job, can't see the Jewish Agency authorities, and can't get into *Amidar*.*"

In the course of the discussions there is occasional reference by physicians to the relationship of sickness to failure: "Patients feel themselves to be failures and come to the doctor to gain strength."

Some doctors refer to the pressure exerted on them by demanding patients. Most physicians prefer to give in to such demands rather than risk trouble from overdemanding patients: "If I don't give him the certificate he wants, he feels I'm against him and preventing him from getting ahead. So I give in." "When I started to work, I was advised by a colleague, 'Give the patient whatever he wants; just be sure to avoid a scandal.'"

In this context it is of some interest to report an additional finding from the patient side of the doctor-patient relationship, on patients' perceptions of physicians' response to their need for obtaining certification of illness. When asked, "Do you find that it is difficult to obtain a *petek?*" non-Europeans reply in the affirmative more frequently than Europeans. The difference between the Rumanians and the Moroccans is significant, with the latter reporting more difficulty in obtaining legitimation for illness. This finding fits into the general picture that emerges in this chapter: of greater need for legitimation of illness by the non-Europeans, perception by physicians of the non-Europeans as high demanders of legitimation and possibly as malingerers, less willingness on the part of physicians to respond positively to this need of the non-European patients, and comparatively widespread feeling by these patients that it is not easy to get the doctor to grant the desired legitimation. Clearly there is a measure of circularity in this process.

SUMMARY

This chapter has concerned itself with legitimation of illness as a latent function of the medical institution. We have proposed

* *Amidar* is the National Housing Authority.

that illness may represent one way of coping with failure and that the physician plays a unique role as the sole authority granting that legitimation. In contrast to the other needs discussed, the present one can find satisfaction only within a medical context. For people of limited means or incomplete knowledge of and access to the medical alternatives, Kupat Holim may in fact serve as the only locus for obtaining legitimation of illness. Such a situation places a special burden on the physician particularly in a context of immigration in which feelings of failure could be fairly widespread in the population.

While about half of the population studied expresses a feeling of failure in two or more of the four areas observed, the frequency of this feeling does not vary too much among the ethnic groups although there is some evidence to indicate that the Rumanians feel less failure than the other groups. We know that objective, situational factors differ among the ethnic groups—especially between the European and non-European populations—but these differences do not seem to be reflected too clearly in the subjective level of failure expressed. Such a finding reaffirms the importance of apparent subjective elements in conditioning people's response to what may be widely different objective situations.

Non-Europeans tend more than the Europeans to believe that formal certification of illness represents a central function of Kupat Holim. We have noted that non-Europeans may in fact find themselves in more frequent need of such certification because of extramedical institutional requirements which make the *petek* a prerequisite for obtaining certain rewards and privileges which Europeans can more easily obtain without formal certification.

Nevertheless, testing the hypothesis on coping with failure by means of respondents' perception of the importance of the *petek* in Kupat Holim fails to show systematic confirmation. Although the rural Moroccans show confirmation of the hypothesis, none of the other groups do, and our conclusion must therefore be a conservative one: there is no evidence for general confirmation of the hypothesis when perception of the centrality of the *petek* is used as the dependent variable. When, on the other hand, we use frequency of clinic attendance as the dependent variable we find consistent confirmation of the hypothesis in all ethnic groups as well as in

almost all of their subgroups. Furthermore this confirmation holds
when we divide the population into sick and healthy sectors. These
findings point to the operation of the latent function and provide a
strong basis to believe that high clinic utilization is at least partly a
result of clients' seeking to enjoy the latent function.

It will be recalled that we pointed to the difficulty of defining acceptable dependent variables for testing the legitimation of
failure hypothesis. The difficulty is particularly severe on the perception and attitudinal level. For in a sense the most reasonable
dependent variable is a behavioral one: actual attendance. This is
the case because coming to the physician's office by definition implies the desire to obtain professional legitimation for entry into the
sick role. For this reason confirmation of the hypothesis among
respondents who define themselves as healthy is an extremely interesting finding, which points to the fruitfulness of the theoretical
formulation we have proposed.

When we turn to physicians' response patterns, a number of
fruitful findings emerge. Physicians tend to believe that Moroccans
are considerably more likely than Rumanians to become sick and
to seek legitimation for such illness as a response to some sort of
failure in their everyday lives. In fact we know that Moroccans
feel failure somewhat more frequently than Rumanians. There is a
strong and clear difference between physicians' image of the two
ethnic groups in this area. There is also evidence that doctors
respond to Moroccan patients of this sort with less sympathy and
understanding than to Rumanian patients. While they claim to give
equal *medical* care to members of both groups, we have raised the
question of whether this is indeed likely when their attitudes and
orientations toward the two ethnic groups are demonstrably so
different. In order to carry out the universalistic professional ideal
of similar treatment, it would be necessary for physicians to maintain a strong system of insulation between their professional norms
and other attitudes and orientations which characterize them.

There appears to be a certain invidious quality in the doctor-
patient relationship described here. Non-European patients report
more difficulty than Europeans in obtaining formal certification
of illness from the Kupat Holim physician. Taken together with
our findings on the differential perception and orientation of physi-

cians to the two ethnic groups, we are led to surmise that the comparative difficulty reported by the non-Europeans may in fact be a real one and could reflect physicians' resentment and possible lack of sympathy toward patients who are perceived as potential malingerers and who demand more than what is thought to be their appropriate share of legitimation of illness. Since non-Europeans state more frequently than Europeans that *petek*-granting is a central function of the Kupat Holim clinic, it would seem reasonable to assume that they do in fact request certifications more often than their European counterparts. We have suggested that this excessive demand may reflect a need imposed by nonmedical bureaucratic structures in the society which make these certifications conditional for obtaining certain desired rewards. Be the reason what it may, the excessive demand by the non-Europeans reinforces physicians' perception of this group as unreasonably high demanders of certification. This reaction tends to produce a measure of hostility and a need to avoid being exploited by malingerers.

8

Integration into Israel

As a veteran, well-established, and prominently known Israeli institution, Kupat Holim is in an unusual position to assist its immigrant members in the process of entry into Israeli society. Its association with the powerful Histadrut (Federation of Labor) serves to emphasize its integral association with the dominant establishment. Interestingly enough, Kupat Holim recognizes this latent function and refers to it in one of its information pamphlets: "Kupat Holim plays an important role in immigrants' integration and in merging different groups by means of the same kind of medical aid to newcomers and old settlers alike, and by providing equal treatment to all members both from advanced and backward countries" (Kanev, 1965, p. 15).

What is most suggestive in this statement is the reference to a universalistic orientation of the medical institution as a factor contributing to the integration process. From a sociological point of view this element in the orientation of the physician, who is the most visible representative of the institution, might well be salient to the integration process. Such a universalistic orientation could be especially important for non-European immigrants, who encounter or perceive prejudice, who do not have ready access to alternative institutions where they can enjoy a universalistic orientation of personnel toward them (Shuval, 1955, 1956, 1962a, 1962b, 1966, 1967).

There are fairly strong pressures within the Kupat Holim structure which push physicians to a universalistic orientation. Norms of the medical profession are strongly universalistic, requiring an orientation that ignores characteristics of the patient that are medically irrelevant and considers all patients as patients regardless of differences among them. In addition to these professional norms, the Kupat Holim physician is subject to certain universalistic bureaucratic norms which govern the relations of staff members of large medical bureaucracies to clients. Finally, Kupat Holim is part of the Histadrut and as a veteran Israeli institution undoubtedly accepts and needs to find expression for those equalitarian norms which are central to the official norms of the society.

These several lines of pressure would tend to strengthen the physician's universalistic orientation patterns and possibly make him less open than others in expressing the mild but widespread prejudice that exists in Israeli society. This is not to argue that he is personally immune, but rather that he is supported by several sets of forces which stem from different institutional sources and which act in the same general direction.

How does an immigrant move into Israeli society and what role does the medical institution play in this process? Clearly there are many channels of entry and different channels will be selected by various types of immigrants depending on need and background.

One way of looking at the process of entry is in terms of a gradual shedding of an immigrant's ethnic identity until he perceives himself and is perceived by others as an Israeli rather than as a member of a specific ethnic group. In a society composed of immigrants from many different ethnic backgrounds, a newly arrived immigrant is perceived and categorized largely in terms of his ethnic origin. Different customs and behavior patterns which heighten visibility make this inevitable. With time many ethnic characteristics are modified—for example, language, dress, food habits—until the immigrant becomes unidentifiable as a member of an ethnic group and is seen as an Israeli. This process may take months, years, or generations.

From this point of view an immigrant with continuing tenacious attachments to his ethnic group is slowing down his process of entry into Israeli society. Reinforcement of internal ethnic bonds heightens the individual's visibility and identifiability as a member of an ethnic group and slows down his transformation into an Israeli. These considerations do not weigh the comparative desirability of rapid or gradual shedding of ethnic identity by immigrants. It is entirely feasible that gradual disengagement from traditional ethnic patterns may be more favorable to long-term adjustment and acculturation than rapid change. The point here is that one mechanism of entry and integration into Israeli society is through a shedding of ethnic identity.

We have already suggested that this process may be easier for Europeans than for non-Europeans. One reason lies in the greater congruence with dominant Israeli values of European culture patterns brought by such immigrants. Another could be associated with stronger traditional group or extended family ties of non-European immigrants which cause them to persist longer in their ethnic identification patterns. But among the more important factors might well be the patterns of resistance and stereotyping that could be encountered or perceived in Israeli society by non-European immigrants. While the society is basically an open one, there is reason to believe that non-Europeans may have somewhat greater difficulty moving upward in the established channels of mobility. This is partly a result of their lower level of education and relatively deprived social background, but it could also be related to attitudes and orientations of European members of the society toward them. In Israel, as in many societies, there is a relationship between ethnic origin and class position, with the non-European segments of the population clustering more heavily at the lower end of the class continuum. Failure to move upward in the class hierarchy thus results in a reinforcement of one's ethnic identity as well (Hanoch, 1961).

It is from this point of view that a medical institution such as Kupat Holim may play a role in the integration process. Immigrants characterized by a need to drop their ethnic identity and move as Israelis into the broader ranges of the social system would be likely to seek out social contexts in which the orientation of others toward them would not be in terms of ethnic categorizations. While there are pressures toward universalistic patterns of orientation of personnel toward clients in many bureaucratic settings, few outside of Kupat Holim are characterized by as many structurally built-in forces pressuring toward such a pattern of universalistic orientations. Furthermore, as pointed out earlier, few institutional contexts are as easily available and accessible to the public.

In sum, immigrants from non-European countries who want to lose their ethnic identity and be related to as Israelis might be likely to encounter difficulties in attaining this goal in many segments of Israeli society. The considerations spelled out above lead us to expect that this group would be most likely to seek out the Kupat Holim context as a means for satisfying this need. Suchman (1964, 1966) proposes that "ethnic exclusivity" will be associated with a less positive orientation to a Western medical context. It is in this sense that we speak of Kupat Holim playing a role in the integration of immigrants into Israeli society. In contrast to the other latent functions considered, our analysis makes this one applicable especially to the non-Europeans in our population so that the hypothesis applies only to them. Reformulated in more sociological terms, the idea behind our thinking seems to parallel the notion stated in the Kupat Holim publication quoted above (Kanev, 1965).

OVERVIEW OF VARIABLES

The need for integration *into* Israeli society has been defined in terms of respondents' desire to move *out of* their original ethnic group. The items defining the scale on need for integration were based on respondents' stated interest in contacts with people outside their own ethnic group. Such contact focused on areas of personal friendship, children's friendships, and work relations.

Our findings reveal few differences in the level of this need among Moroccan, Kurdish and Polish subjects; the Rumanians, however, appear considerably lower than the other three groups in their need for integration. Such a patterning indicates that there are no major cross-ethnic elements at work but rather something associated with the Rumanians per se.

A more detailed look at the subgroups composing the population indicates that a low need for integration is not general to the Rumanians but appears principally among the urban Rumanians. This need is especially low among the urban Rumanian women and the older, less educated respondents in this subgroup. It will be recalled that this group is older on the average than the other groups in the study. But even other segments of the urban Rumanian population are low in the need for integration. We will have occasion to return to this finding when we discuss physicians' response to the need for integration later in this chapter. Other than the above, the detailed analysis of this set of findings shows no subgroups in the other ethnic-residential groups in which the need for integration is consistently high or low.

Some difficulty was encountered in designing questions that could be considered valid measures for clients' perceived satisfaction of the need for integration by Kupat Holim. This difficulty is associated with Israeli norms which pressure against open reference to differential orientations in ethnic terms. After several experiments with a variety of formulations, it was found most effective to question respondents on whether they feel that Kupat Holim personnel behave differently to old-time Israeli patients and to patients of the respondent's country of origin. The deliberately ambiguous concept, "behave differently" was selected in order to focus on the universalistic element of personnel orientation toward clients. The three items, which referred in turn to physicians, administrative personnel, and nurses, defined a Guttman scale. It was therefore possible to trichotomize the scale continuum into groups which perceive Kupat Holim personnel as (1) not ethnically oriented to clients, that is, most universalistic, (2) mixed in their orientation on this dimension, and (3) ethnically oriented to clients, that is, least universalistic in their orientation to clients.

Our findings about the differences among the four ethnic

groups of respondents on this variable indicate that the Moroccans and Kurds have a similar patterning: about half perceive Kupat Holim personnel as non-ethnically oriented and approximately a fifth perceive them to be ethnically oriented. The Rumanians show the highest frequency of all four groups in perceiving Kupat Holim personnel as ethnically oriented, a point of considerable interest in view of the low need for integration reported above. A statistical examination shows that these two variables are related among the Rumanians: low need for integration is associated with perception of Kupat Holim personnel as non-universalistically oriented. It is entirely feasible that the Rumanians feel that an ethnic orientation on the part of Kupat Holim personnel is a desirable pattern insofar as they are concerned—a possible example of "positive prejudice." The small number of people characterized by a high need for integration among the Rumanians makes it statistically impossible to control on a sufficient number of relevant variables in order to push this analysis much further. The Poles are highest in their perception of Kupat Holim personnel as non-ethnically oriented. A breakdown into subgroups confirms these findings. Among the non-Europeans there is also some tendency for younger respondents to be less likely to perceive Kupat Holim personnel as non-ethnically oriented. The latter trend does not appear, however, among the Europeans with any consistency.

INTEGRATION HYPOTHESIS

The integration hypothesis is confirmed when we look at the total population in Table 13. The critical group shows a more frequent tendency to perceive Kupat Holim personnel as universalistic, that is, non-ethnically oriented, in their relationships to clients. However, we find on closer examination of the ethnic and residential subgroups that the hypothesis is in fact confirmed only among the Moroccans and Kurds. This finding is further substantiated when we break the ethnic-residential groups into subgroups defined by sex, age, and education. Virtually all such subgroups among the Moroccans and Kurds show a general confirmation of the hypothesis while this patterning fails to appear with any consistency among the Europeans.

This differential pattern of the ethnic groups confirms our

Table 13

Perception of Kupat Holim Personnel

Need for Integration, Tendency to Define Oneself as Ill	Percentage of clients who perceive Kupat Holim personnel as:			N
	Non-ethnically Oriented	Mixed in their Orientation	Ethnically Oriented	
High need, high tendency	67[a]	17	16	527
High need, low tendency	62	18	19	371
Low need, high tendency	52	22	26	482
Low need, low tendency	43	19	37	454

[a] The difference between the critical group and the other three groups combined is significant. $X^2 = 40.81$, D.F. $= 2$, P $< .001$.

prediction and we may therefore conclude that Moroccan and Kurdish clients with a high need to move out of the confines of their ethnic group and with a tendency to define themselves as ill, do reveal the expected pattern of perception of Kupat Holim personnel: a pattern which highlights the universalistic, non-ethnically oriented quality of Kupat Holim personnel toward them. While we do not have data available on these clients' experiences and perceptions of other institutions, it would seem reasonable to suggest that the medical institution is satisfying a certain need of these clients and in this manner is contributing in some way to their integration into Israeli society. For them this latent function is operating.

While the critical group reveals a particularly high frequency in perceiving Kupat Holim personnel as non-ethnically oriented, there is no evidence that perception of this latent function carries behavioral consequences, at least insofar as frequency of clinic attendance is concerned. Section A of Table 14 shows that the tendency to define oneself as ill is associated with more frequent physician utilization, but high frequency of attendance is not concentrated in the critical group. This generalization holds regardless of clients' perception of Kupat Holim personnel as non-ethnically oriented or as ethnically oriented. It also holds when we examine the patterning for Europeans and non-Europeans separately. Despite the tendency of the critical group to highlight the universalistic orientation of Kupat Holim personnel on a *perception* level, it does not engage in especially frequent clinic-utilization in a possible attempt to enjoy this latent function on a *behavioral* level. There is therefore no basis to assume that high utilization rates are a result of clients' desire to enjoy this latent function.

There is evidence from Sections B and C of Table 14 that people who perceive Kupat Holim personnel as non-ethnically oriented are more satisfied with the medical services of the institution and tend more frequently to exclusive use of Kupat Holim facilities. Both of these findings point to greater general satisfaction on the part of clients who sense the universalistic qualities of Kupat Holim personnel. Such findings tend to confirm the point noted by Coady (1955) concerning the positive aspects of clinic "anonymity."

Table 14

UTILIZATION AND ATTITUDE PATTERNS TOWARD KUPAT HOLIM
(Integration Hypothesis)

Need for Integration, Tendency to Define Oneself as Ill	A — Percentage who report 20 or more visits a year to Kupat Holim doctor — Perceive Kupat Holim personnel as:[a]		B — Percentage who report themselves satisfied with medical care of Kupat Holim — Perceive Kupat Holim personnel as:		C — Percentage who use only Kupat Holim, do not use private or other clinics — Perceive Kupat Holim personnel as:	
	Non-ethnically oriented	Ethnically oriented	Non-ethnically oriented	Ethnically oriented	Non-ethnically oriented	Ethnically oriented
High need, high tendency	18 (349)	14 (81)	77 (342)	54 (82)	86 (352)	74 (82)
High need, low tendency	9 (225)	8 (72)	67 (224)	58 (71)	81 (225)	71 (70)
Low need, high tendency	22 (236)	22 (124)	73 (245)	61 (121)	81 (242)	71 (111)
Low need, low tendency	7 (191)	11 (168)	72 (193)	58 (161)	71 (195)	70 (154)

[a] This table includes the extremes of the population only, that is, those who perceive Kupat Holim personnel as clearly non-ethnically oriented or clearly ethnically oriented. The middle group who perceive Kupat Holim personnel as mixed in their orientation are not included here. See Table 13.

However we do not find that the critical group shows especially high satisfaction with the medical services of Kupat Holim nor does it report more exclusive use of Kupat Holim services than other groups in the population. This is in line with our findings from Section A of Table 14, which show no clear-cut behavioral consequences in the critical group of satisfying the need for integration through perception of Kupat Holim personnel as universalistic in their orientations to clients. Again we examined these relationships separately among European and non-European clients and the same generalizations hold.

To summarize: Non-European clients characterized by a high need for integration and a high tendency to define themselves as ill show a uniquely high frequency in perceiving Kupat Holim personnel as non-ethnically oriented toward them. In line with our hypothesis, we have interpreted this finding to mean that these clients are gaining certain rewards from the medical institution through such a pattern of perception by satisfying a need to enjoy universalistic, non-ethnically oriented relations with official personnel of Israeli institutions. In this sense it appears that Kupat Holim is playing some part in furthering the integration of these immigrants into Israeli society.

At the same time it appears that satisfaction of this need in terms of such a pattern of perception does not result in more frequent attendance at the Kupat Holim clinic nor does the critical group show uniquely high general satisfaction as indicated by attitudes toward Kupat Holim personnel and extent of exclusive use of Kupat Holim facilities.

PHYSICIANS' RESPONSE

Physicians are characterized by different attitudes and beliefs concerning immigrants' efforts to move actively into Israeli society. Such differences could be associated with their image of the appropriate role pattern of the physician in Israel: as an active socializer of immigrants who can and should be taught not only appropriate health measures but also given auxiliary information, or as a more narrowly defined professional who should limit his role to strictly medically relevant matters (Morag, 1966).

Following the approach taken in the analysis of the patient

population, we have considered physicians' responses to the need for integration in terms of his attitude toward patients' desire to move out of the confines of their ethnic group membership. It will be recalled that moving out of this framework was viewed as an attempt to move into the broader ranges of Israeli society. The question considered now is: to what extent do physicians support such efforts in their patient population and how do they respond when they encounter them? Do physicians respond differently in this area to their European and non-European clients?

The empirical approach we have taken is based on the assumption that overt attempts by the physician to pressure patients to give up traditional, ethnically-oriented customs and behavior patterns represents *support* for those immigrants who desire to move out of the traditional ethnic environment and into the wider ranges of Israeli society. While in a sense such pressure by the physician can be viewed as critical and possibly frustrating to those clients characterized by a need for integration, it would still seem to provide a certain basic satisfaction of this need. If the physician's attitude is expressed in a positive context. ("I am glad to see how much progress you have made in speaking Hebrew and that you no longer talk Arabic," "I'm pleased that you have given up traditional customs of medical treatment," and so on), it is quite clearly rewarding and supportive of the need for integration. When it is formulated negatively or more critically ("I wish you would stop speaking Arabic and use Hebrew," "You must stop using traditional customs of medical treatment"), it contains a larger dose of frustration but can still be thought of as supporting the need for integration among clients characterized by such a need because it lends a certain weight, authority and legitimation to their efforts in this direction. In any case the argument is a relative rather than an absolute one: clients with a need for integration will be *more* satisfied by physicians who encourage them to drop traditional ethnic customs than will clients with a low need for integration and a greater desire to remain within the confines of their ethnic group. The latter are more likely to perceive such attitudes of the physician as critical. An exception to this generalization could occur among clients characterized by a high need for integration but who, despite desire and effort, are not successful in their efforts to move out of their ethnic group. We refer, for example, to immigrants who would like to speak Hebrew or feel they should speak Hebrew, but are unable to master the language. Speaking their native language might in such cases be accompanied by a sense of failure or guilt. A critical attitude by the physician which points up this failure and encourages more integrated performance could under such circumstances heighten the individual's feeling of guilt and inadequacy. However, while this configuration certainly cannot be considered maximally supportive on the part of the physician, it might still be *relatively* supportive if we compare this subgroup with respondents characterized by a low need for integration who would be fundamentally frustrated by physicians who pressure them to abandon traditional, ethnic-oriented patterns.

Three questions were posed to physicians, one focusing on traditional medical practices, and the other two on more general ethnocentric patterns:

a. Let us assume that one of your Moroccan (or Rumanian) patients tells you that he uses a traditional home remedy which has always been used in his country of origin. You know that this remedy has no pharmacological effect, either positive or negative. If he were to ask your opinion about this, what would you advise him?

   1. I would advise him to stop using it.
   2. I would avoid giving advice.
   3. I would tell him he could continue using it if he wanted to.

b. What is your opinion of Moroccan (or Rumanian) parents who continue to speak their mother tongue with their children after they have been in Israel for several years?

   1. I think this practice is desirable.
   2. This practice is undesirable but can't be prevented.
   3. This practice is not so desirable.

c. There are many Moroccan (or Rumanian) immigrants who continue to prefer friends from their own ethnic group even after they have been in Israel for several years. What is your opinion of this?

   1. I think this practice is desirable.

2. This practice is undesirable but can't be prevented.

3. I think this practice is not so desirable.

The findings yielded a rather different empirical picture for the item relating to "medical integration" than for the two items referring to more general, non-health-related areas. On the whole physicians appear more concerned to stop patients of both ethnic groups from using traditional medical remedies, even—as stated explicitly in the question—when this practice is in no way damaging from a medical point of view. Half or more of the physicians feel that such traditional practices should be eliminated while only a quarter disapprove the use of respondents' mother tongue or of ethnocentric friendships. Physicians apparently feel that traditional medical practices fall quite clearly within the realm of their medical practice and concern while other ethnocentric practices do not. Professional concern therefore leads to a more active integrating or socializing role within the area perceived as relevant to medical practice but does not generalize to areas viewed as outside that realm. (This general comparison should be viewed with some reservation because the cutting points used in each item are in a sense arbitrary. Nevertheless the findings are suggestive.)

In addition, the doctors may believe that a specific non-Western medical practice, even if in itself not harmful, could be accompanied by other traditional practices or beliefs which might be harmful or which might prevent the use by such patients of more acceptable Western medical procedures. In a more general sense these physicians might believe that Western medicine cannot tolerate parallel systems of therapy based on a different cultural rationale.

The second finding concerns the differential attitude of physicians to Rumanian and Moroccan patients who continue to use a traditional remedy. We find a significant difference in physicians' orientation to these two ethnic groups, with a more integrating attitude expressed toward the Rumanians, that is, doctors are more likely to advise a Rumanian than a Moroccan patient to give up using a traditional medical practice. There are no significant differences between physicians' attitudes toward the two ethnic groups of patients with respect to the other items observed.

An examination of subgroups of physicians in terms of sex, age, ethnic origin, and seniority in the profession shows no significant differences among these groups in the response to patients' need for integration.

These findings are doubly interesting in the light of our data concerning the relative need for integration of the two ethnic groups of clients. It will be recalled that the Rumanians show a remarkably low frequency of need for integration as measured in this study, while this need is expressed with greater frequency by the Moroccans. The need as expressed by the clients themselves is greater among those to whom physicians respond less positively (Moroccans), and least among those to whom physician response is more integrative (Rumanians). While we are unable to judge the extent of client satisfaction in terms of the absolute level of physician behavior, the reversal is certainly striking.

Our guess is that the differential pattern of physician orientation to the two ethnic groups can be explained at least partially in terms of the former's expectations with respect to these clients. The comparatively higher level of education of the Rumanians and their greater cultural closeness to the physicians themselves lead the doctors to expect such patients to behave more in conformity with the norms of Western medical practice. If clients deviate from such norms—as in the situation posed by our question on traditional medical practice—they should certainly be pressured back into line, for such practices are not viewed as appropriate for such people. At the same time a greater tolerance can be permitted of Moroccans, who are seen as less educated and sophisticated; they may therefore be permitted with greater frequency to persist in such traditional medical practices. Tolerance of this sort can be viewed as a sort of condescension toward the "unsophisticated" group in that it suggests they are not quite as ready to become socialized into a more modern culture context.

There is a good deal of evidence in the doctors' discussions for this view of the Moroccans. They are perceived as primitive and this is seen as disturbing to their role as patients: "Immigrants from North Africa are uncultured and have no understanding of what we tell them. We have no common language." "These Moroccan immigrants can't give you a clear answer to the simplest question. When I ask how long he has had this pain, he replies, for a long time. How long—years? No. Months? No. It finally turns out that he's had it for two days."

Although there is an awareness of the need to educate patients, doctors feel that such people are not that easy to educate. Not only is communication with them a problem but they often engage in physically threatening behavior: "We can't even talk to these patients. They don't speak anything but Arabic and they don't understand." "Lots of these patients come in armed with knives and threaten us if we don't give them what they want."

Nevertheless, listening to the doctors talk, one comes away with the impression that many members of this profession possess a deep belief in the importance and potential of education, even if they are not entirely clear on how it is to be accomplished: "All these problems depend on education of the patient. As I look back on my practice, I know that whatever I have achieved has been through educating my patients." "Education of patients would solve a lot of problems. Even if they are illiterate and come from uncultured backgrounds, they need to be taught." "We use all sorts of childish methods to make sure the patient understands. For example, we tell him to take red pills for this, and green pills for that. And then we ask him to repeat the instructions to make sure he understands." "People have to be taught that they don't have to run to the clinic for every running nose or headache." "Patients must be taught discipline and if they come from poor backgrounds, we have to teach them."

SUMMARY

We have proposed in this chapter that Kupat Holim may play a role in the integration of immigrants into Israeli society. It would seem that this role is particularly appropriate for certain of the non-European members of Kupat Holim who may enjoy the clinic situation and the universalistic, non-ethnically oriented approach of Kupat Holim personnel to its clients. In fact, the empirical test of this hypothesis shows it to be confirmed for the non-European groups in our population: non-Europeans with a high need to become integrated into Israeli society and a high tendency to define themselves as ill (the critical group) report more frequently than others that Kupat Holim personnel do *not* relate to them in ethnic terms. We have taken this finding to mean that these people, who are characterized by a high need to drop their ethnic identity, succeed comparatively frequently in satisfying this need within the framework of the medical institution. This pattern thus represents a certain enjoyment of this latent function by those segments of the non-European population with an appropriate need.

Enjoyment of the latent function is, however, limited to clients' perception. There is no evidence that the critical group visits the clinic physician with especially high frequency. Nor does this perceptual enjoyment of the latent function express itself in terms of greater satisfaction with medical care provided by Kupat Holim or in less frequent utilization of non-Kupat Holim medical facilities, that is, in more exclusive reliance on the facilities provided by Kupat Holim.

It is therefore inappropriate to argue that enjoyment of this latent function is contributing to the high utilization rates of Kupat Holim clinics. However, attitudes of the non-European members of Kupat Holim do indicate that the institution is playing a certain integrative role for them in providing a context in which they can enjoy a type of attitude and orientation from the personnel which they need or desire.

When we looked at the opposite side of the coin in terms of physicians' response to patients' need for integration, we did not find a pattern of complementarity. Rumanian patients who show a comparatively low need for integration are accorded a relatively positive response by physicians in terms of support for such integration. Moroccans, on the other hand, are characterized by a higher need than Rumanians for integration into Israeli society, but are responded to less positively by the Kupat Holim physicians. We suggested that the latter may be responding to the two ethnic groups in terms of different sets of expectations: Rumanians because of their higher average level of education and their greater cultural similarity to the doctors themselves, are expected to conform more closely to a Western patient role and therefore to avoid traditional remedies of the sort that are not prescribed by the Western physician. Physicians therefore feel justified in exerting pressure on Rumanians when they do in fact engage in such traditional practices. Such pressure is less frequently exerted on Moroccans who engage in traditional medical practices, possibly because such "unsophisticated" behavior on their part is more generally expected.

We have also noted that physicians are more likely to undertake an integrative role in areas directly relevant to medicine than in other areas. When questioned about ethnocentric behavior in nonmedical areas they show less willingness to exert pressure on their clients to give up practices that tend to impede entry into the broader ranges of Israeli society. To the extent that they engage in integrative behavior, it is medically specific, rather than diffusely oriented. In this sense they cannot be considered "socializers" in any but a strictly medical context.

9

Gaining Status

The status hypothesis is based on the assumption that physicians in Israel occupy a relatively high status position. Although no systematic study has established this fact in Israel to date, there is evidence from many countries with diversified social systems that doctors are generally ranked well at the top of the hierarchy of occupations (Bendix and Lipset, 1966; Feldman, 1966; Inkeles and Rossi, 1956). Many of the reasons for this high status elsewhere would seem to apply to Israel: first, the relatively long period of academic training required for the profession—a fact which generally is associated with high occupational prestige; second, the association of the medical profession with science and its values, which are held in generally high esteem in Israeli society, as well as with research and its aura of prestige; third, the superordinate position of the physician in his contacts with people in the patient role; and fourth, the high value placed by Israeli society on health. The latter may be partly an outgrowth of East European Jewish attitudes toward health (Zborowski and Herzog, 1952) and partly

144

a matter of national concern with the physical well-being of the nation during a period of early consolidation. It may also reflect a concern to maintain a Western standard of living in the country.

On the assumption that the physician occupies a relatively high status position in the society, the hypothesis proposes that clients with a high need for status and a tendency to define themselves as ill will take advantage of this high status. More than the other subgroups, they will attempt to gain some of the status of the physician through contact with him. Gans (1962) has noted that West Enders perceive the hospital and its personnel as "of extremely high status, endowed with economic and political influence of gargantuan proportions" (pp. 137–138). This is accomplished when the physician conforms to his ideal role with regard to a universalistic orientation and shows respect and tolerance for the patient's background and needs so that he may give clients a feeling of status gained through association. A personal interest in the patient by the high-status physician could establish a sort of equalitarian relationship—which might be highly rewarding to clients with a particular need for such rewards.

We have already noted that an equalitarian norm is comparatively strong in Israeli society. This norm tends to attenuate—without abolishing—the status gap between physician and patient and possibly permits the patient to gain status through contact with the physician more than he would in a society in which such a norm is absent or weaker. The rewards of such contact may be reaped when the subject reports to salient reference groups about his visit to the doctor. Or the rewards may be internal as the client reflects on his visit to such a prestigeful person.

This latent function will be activated, of course, only if the physician does not depart too far from his ideal role. If, for example, he emphasizes the status gap between himself and his client too strongly, the opposite effect may result. Intolerance, lack of patience, or lack of respect for the patient may boomerang to give the client a lesser feeling of status.

OVERVIEW OF VARIABLES

The need for status is defined in terms of the difference between the respondent's own level of education and the level of education he now thinks important for a person of his sort. The latter was estimated by means of a question which posed a hypothetical situation of a boy, of average ability, from a socio-economic background similar to that of the respondent, who just finished eighth grade. Respondents were asked how many years and what sort of education they would recommend for this boy. Possible responses included the opinion that eight years of school are enough, trade school, high school without matriculation certificate, matriculation, and university education.

This procedure is meaningful against a social background in which free compulsory education covers only the first nine grades. While there are graded tuition fees for secondary school in accordance with family income, neither secondary school nor higher education is free in Israel. A free compulsory tenth year of education will probably be instituted in the near future and additional free schooling is also likely in the not too distant future. For people who themselves completed only eight grades or less, the belief that some high school is necessary—even without a matriculation certificate—represents a certain unwillingness to accept the inevitable lower status that a limited education implies and a desire to attain a higher position in the social system. The same is true of people who themselves attended high school but believe that a university education is important for the hypothetical boy. In both cases we assume a certain status sensitivity and desire for mobility. On the other hand, respondents who state that the hypothetical boy requires a level of education equal to or lower than their own are presumably characterized by less status sensitivity and less of a need for mobility.

In sum, respondents were characterized by a high need for status if there was a gap of several years between their own level of education and the level they considered necessary for the hypothetical boy. They were characterized as low in their need for status if this gap was small, negative, or nonexistent. Need for status was determined by a cross-tabulation of respondent's own education and proposed education of the hypothetical boy as follows: *High need for status:* respondents who themselves had no formal schooling or less than eight years of school and who stated the hypothetical boy should have at least some high school; respondents who themselves completed eight grades, *yeshiva* (religious school), or trade school and who stated that the hypothetical boy should have at least a high school matriculation certificate; respondents who themselves completed high school with a matriculation certificate and stated that the hypothetical boy should continue to the university. *Low need for status:* all others (with the exception of those who stated that the hypothetical boy should also attend university). This definition does not consider intensity of need for status nor does it take into account different sizes of the gap between respondent's own education and the level he considers important for the hypothetical boy.

Comparison of the ethnic groups on need for status shows that over half of the Kurds and Moroccans as contrasted to a third or less of the European groups are high on this need. However, the nature of the definition of need for status places a certain "ceiling effect" on this variable. This is because there are more possible choices open to less educated respondents than there are for more educated respondents to indicate a higher level of education than their own for the hypothetical boy. Among the two non-European groups high need for status appears to be somewhat more heavily concentrated in the younger subgroups and among the rural as contrasted to the urban Kurds. Among the Rumanians and Poles this need is found more frequently in the less educated segments of the population.

The dependent variable is defined in terms of respondents' perception of the comparative prestige of the Kupat Holim physician. Activation of the latent function as we have defined it requires that clients perceive the clinic physician as a high status professional. Only under such circumstances can they hope to gain status through association with him and with the institution he represents. While perception alone does not indicate the extent to which they succeed in gaining such status—because it does not consider the nature of the physician's response to clients—it would appear to be a necessary first step to activation of the status-giving latent function: unless clients perceive the physician as relatively high in status, this latent function cannot even begin to operate. In a sense we may think of this dependent variable as defining the institution's perceived potential for activating the latent function.

The comparative status of the Kupat Holim physician was defined in terms of a set of questions in each of which the Kupat Holim physician was compared in status to another occupation: engineer, lawyer, high government official, and high school principal. Four comparatively high-ranking occupations were deliberately chosen for this comparison. To compare a physician in Israel —or in most Western societies—to middle- or low-ranking occupations provides little, if any, variation in response. The resulting Guttman scale was trichotomized as follows: those who felt that the physician ranks higher in prestige than all of the others, those who gave mixed answers concerning the comparative status of these occupations, and those who felt that all four rank higher than the Kupat Holim physician. Clearly we are dealing with the comparative status of the Kupat Holim physician rather than with his absolute status.

The ethnic groups do not differ much in their perception of the comparative status of the Kupat Holim physician. However, there is a suggestion that the Moroccans and Kurds perceive him as somewhat higher in status than the two European groups. It will be recalled that these groups are also characterized by a relatively high need for status. Closer observation in terms of age, sex, and level of education categories of the ethnic groups shows that it is essentially the older and less educated subgroups of the non-Europeans who most frequently perceive the Kupat Holim physician as high in status.

STATUS HYPOTHESIS

Table 15 presents the formal test of the status hypothesis and shows it to be confirmed: members of the critical group most frequently perceive the Kupat Holim physician to be high in status. However, a more detailed examination of the hypothesis shows it to be confirmed only in certain specific subgroups of the population.

The first of these consists of older, less educated, female subgroups of the urban and rural Kurds. These are the least acculturated, most tradition-bound subgroups of the most traditional ethnic group in the study. The remaining Kurds and the Moroccans, urban and rural, do not confirm the hypothesis.

This picture indicates that those segments of the non-Euro-

Table 15

CLIENTS' PERCEPTION OF PHYSICIAN STATUS

Need for Status, Tendency to Define Oneself as Ill	Percentage of clients who perceive Kupat Holim physician's relative status as:			
	High	Medium	Low	N
High need, high tendency[a]	45	46	9	479
High need, low tendency	33	51	16	314
Low need, high tendency	36	48	16	523
Low need, low tendency	29	56	15	502

[a] The difference between the critical group and all of the other groups combined is significant. $X^2 = 30.31$, D.F. $= 2$, $P < .001$.

pean population which are attempting to move more actively out of the traditional culture and into Israeli society do not confirm the hypothesis, that is, the critical subgroup among them does not perceive the physician as particularly prestigeful any more than do other subgroups. This does not mean, of course, that they do not seek elsewhere in the social structure for satisfaction of their need for status, but that the Kupat Holim physician does not possess the prerequisites of status necessary to fill this need.

The failure of the Moroccans to show confirmation of the hypothesis in any subgroup would seem to lend support to the above interpretation. It will be recalled that the Moroccans, in contrast to the Kurds, are better educated, employed in more skilled occupations, and are less religious (see Chapter Three). This configuration has strengthened our impression that this group is probably less tradition-bound and seeking more actively than the other non-European groups to move into Israeli society. If it is essentially the less acculturated who confirm the hypothesis, it would seem that few of the Moroccans, including the oldest, least educated, and female segments of the population, are sufficiently attached to the traditional culture and detached from Israeli society to confirm it.

These findings suggest that the status of the Kupat Holim clinic physician may not be as high as we originally thought. There is probably a marked difference between the prestige of hospital physicians or specialists and general practitioners working in the clinics, with the latter occupying a lower rank within the profession. Even the small number of doctors in private practice seem to carry more prestige than the clinic physician. We have gained the impression as the study has progressed that our population of doctors ranks lower than most other physicians, both in its own eyes and in the eyes of its clients.

Several doctors suggested this in the course of the discussion periods: "Sometimes the patient has more respect for the clerk who gets him in to see the doctor than he does for the doctor himself. It's the clerk who has the power to do him a favor in getting him through the long queue while the doctor is only doing his job because he has to." "Most patients look down on the clinic doctor. They feel they own the clinic and want to get what is due them as members. Once he's paid his dues, he feels that I am his employee." "The difference in status between the doctor and his patient seems to be getting smaller all over the world." "Once a patient has the possibility of choosing a private doctor, his respect for the clinic physician goes way down."

We can speculate as to why this is the case. One factor could be related to the impingement of the bureaucratic official's role on the professional role: the paucity of secretarial and other technical assistance compel the Kupat Holim physician to spend a considerable part of his time on such duties. It has also been observed that too easy access by the public to the clinic physician, often with no buffer in the form of a secretary or nurse to filter clients, has the general effect of lowering his status: familiarity breeds contempt both in his own eyes and in the opinion of clients (see Gamson and Schuman, 1963; Simmons, 1958b). Furthermore it is our impression that there is a growing feeling among the more status-sensitive segments of the population that Kupat Holim is a mass-oriented service organization from which one might do well to disassociate oneself. This point of view tends to lower the perceived status of the entire institution—clients and personnel included: "It's true that patients believe that the doctor is God's representative on earth; however, that representative is not the Kupat Holim doctor but rather the private physician."

Although there may be a good deal of respect and esteem for the medical profession as a whole, this esteem may be differentially focused on various types of physicians. There is reason to believe that in the process, the Kupat Holim clinic physician comes out relatively low in comparison to doctors working in other contexts. A comment by a doctor in Beersheba is enlightening: "We have lots of new immigrants from Iraq and North Africa coming into the clinic. During the first three months they're in the country they still keep to the old tradition and are very polite. But once they've been in the country for a while, all this politeness is gone, until they feel there is no difference in status between us."

If the status of the clinic physician is lower than we originally thought, it is understandable that those segments of the population which are most aware of the realities of the social structure and most in contact with Israeli society would not be likely to perceive the doctor as markedly prestigeful, even if they are characterized by a comparatively high need for status and have a tendency to define themselves as ill. We are not suggesting that he is so low in the status hierarchy that clients should necessarily perceive him as especially low in status: such mobile, Israeli-oriented groups will simply fail to confirm the hypothesis, in either direction. On the other hand, the more tradition-bound, less acculturated subgroups, whose image of the physician probably continues to place him somewhat on a pedestal, are more likely to take advantage of the status-giving latent functions.

An additional factor operating in the same direction is the wider status gap that separates the older, female, uneducated subgroups of the Kurds from the physician. From the point of view of such low status groups, the distance up to the position occupied by the doctor may be considerably magnified.

The discussion thus far applies to the non-Europeans. Neither the urban nor rural Rumanians confirm the hypothesis but the small number of cases in the critical groups makes it impossible to examine subgroups among them and they are therefore eliminated from further analysis.

The Poles provide a more striking confirmation of the hypothesis than any of the other groups observed. Detailed analysis shows that all of the subgroups examined provide consistent con-

firmation of this picture. We may conclude that the urban Poles
with a high need for status and a tendency to define themselves as ill
do perceive the physician as a potential locus for activating the
status-giving latent function.

At first glance, these findings would seem to conflict with
those reported with respect to the non-Europeans. It will be recalled
that the Poles are the best educated, least tradition-oriented, and
work at the highest ranking occupations of all of our ethnic groups
(see Chapter Three). They should, by the logic of the interpretation
proposed above, be least likely to perceive the Kupat Holim physician as highly prestigeful. Indeed, we were confounded initially by
this apparently conflicting empirical picture, and are proposing a
post hoc interpretation which is associated with the ethnic composition of the population of physicians.

The proportion of Polish physicians on the staff of Kupat
Holim is higher than any other single ethnic group. In 1961, 29.3
per cent of the Kupat Holim physicians were of Polish origin. The
closest other single ethnic group at this date were the Rumanian
physicians who represented 16.1 per cent of the total. This means
that from the point of view of Polish patients, the image of the
Kupat Holim physician is probably quite heavily weighted in the
direction of a member of their own ethnic group: by chance alone
almost a third of the physicians they would encounter would be
Poles. Furthermore, the Polish physicians on the Kupat Holim staff
immigrated to Israel earlier than the Rumanians and probably
occupy more powerful positions within the Kupat Holim structure,
since newcomers are more likely to be assigned to rural clinics or
less prestigeful posts. Seventeen per cent of the Polish doctors arrived
in Israel before the establishment of the state, while only 6 per cent
of the Rumanian physicians arrived that early. Of the 342 physicians in the study who arrived before the establishment of the state,
32 per cent are from Poland while only 6 per cent are from Rumania. Kupat Holim physicians who arrived during the early years
of the State, from 1948–1956, were also heavily Polish: 26 per cent
of the present staff who arrived during those years are of Polish
origin, while only 9 per cent are of Rumanian (Kupat Holim,
1962).

It is our suggestion that it may be this unique position of the

Polish physician in Kupat Holim that is conditioning the perception of Polish clients. In contrast to the other ethnic groups we have studied, the Poles are more likely to find members of their own ethnic group among physicians enjoying power and status. This reality could so focus their perception and their image of the Kupat Holim physician as to result in confirmation of our hypothesis.

Another factor which might be considered is the cultural context from which the Poles emigrated. Could there be something unique in the cultural background of this group, in their prior experience with doctors and in their image of the profession which would push them toward confirmation of the hypothesis? We are unable to provide a clear-cut answer to this question.

In sum, we have found confirmation of the status hypothesis among less acculturated segments of the Kurdish group and among the Poles. Among these people, individuals characterized by a high need for status and a tendency to define themselves as ill are likely to perceive Kupat Holim as a potential locus for gaining status. We are unable to test the hypothesis in full detail among the Rumanians because of the small number of cases in the critical group.

SOME CONSEQUENCES

In an attempt to learn about some of the consequences of the perception patterns observed, we have further divided each of the four need-tendency groups into those who perceive the Kupat Holim physician as high in status and those who perceive him as low. In this manner we can see whether these groups differ from each other with respect to utilization of Kupat Holim facilities and in terms of more general attitudes toward the medical institution.

If high frequency of clinic utilization is a function of clients' attempts to enjoy the latent function of the medical institution, we would expect those members of the critical group who perceive the clinic physician to be high in status to show the highest frequency of utilization. In the subgroup, high frequency of clinic attendance coupled with high satisfaction would suggest a pattern of enjoying the status-giving latent function. On the other hand, high frequency of attendance among those who perceive the physician as relatively low in status would suggest a ritualistic pattern in which clients visit the clinic repeatedly in the expectation of obtaining satisfaction of their need but do not succeed. The latter pattern could be a result of physicians' failure to carry out the professional role appropriately, possibly through emphasizing the status-gap between doctor and patient excessively.

Table 16 shows this analysis using frequency of clinic attendance, satisfaction with Kupat Holim, and extent of use of non-Kupat Holim facilities as dependent variables. None of our expectations is borne out. People with a high need for status and a high tendency who perceive the Kupat Holim clinic physician as high in status do not differ from the other subgroups in the frequency of their attendance (Section A) or in the level of their general satisfaction with Kupat Holim (Section B). They do tend somewhat more frequently than others to utilize only Kupat Holim facilities rather than private physicians or other clinic facilities. But this appears to be an isolated finding. Thus our data do not provide evidence that Kupat Holim is utilized by its members in an attempt to gain status through contact with high status figures or with a prestigeful institution. We do not have evidence for enjoyment of this latent function nor does the ritualistic pattern of attendance appear.

On a more general level Table 16 indicates that perception of the Kupat Holim physician as high in status is associated with greater satisfaction with the medical institution as well as with greater exclusive utilization of its facilities (Sections B and C). But it is not associated with more frequent clinic attendance (Section A).

PHYSICIAN'S RESPONSE

We turn now to the opposite side of the coin: the physician's response to patients' need for status. It will be recalled that we have already shown that Moroccans are more frequently characterized by a need for high status than Rumanians. There is also a suggestion that Moroccans tend somewhat more frequently to perceive the Kupat Holim physician as comparatively high in status.

Our prediction is that physicians' response to clients will be a function of the latter's ethnic origin and that they will be more likely to accord status to Rumanian than to Moroccan clients. This prediction derives from the size of the status gap between physicians

Table 16

UTILIZATION AND ATTITUDE PATTERNS TOWARD KUPAT HOLIM: STATUS HYPOTHESIS

Need for Status, Tendency to Define Oneself as Ill	A Percentage who report 20 or more visits a year to Kupat Holim doctor		B Percentage who report themselves satisfied with medical care of Kupat Holim		C Percentage who use only Kupat Holim, do not use private or other clinics	
	Perceive Kupat Holim doctor as:		Perceive Kupat Holim doctor as:		Perceive Kupat Holim doctor as:	
	High in status	Medium or low in status	High in status	Medium or low in status	High in status	Medium or low in status
High need, high tendency	24 (211)	21 (248)	74 (215)	66 (257)	91 (214)	74 (262)
High need, low tendency	11 (99)	12 (202)	74 (101)	53 (206)	78 (99)	74 (204)
Low need, high tendency	20 (187)	19 (325)	72 (184)	60 (330)	81 (188)	74 (315)
Low need, low tendency	6 (142)	8 (350)	73 (138)	61 (346)	82 (141)	69 (341)

and clients of different ethnic groups, from different patterns of
patient behavior characterizing patients of different ethnic origin,
as well as from norms of mild but widespread prejudice in the
social system.

We have noted that physicians may either emphasize or
minimize the status gap between themselves and their clients.
Minimizing the status gap by means of friendliness or personal
warmth would tend to give patients a feeling of closeness. To be
close to the high-status physician and to have him relate to them in
a relatively egalitarian manner could contribute to the status needs
of clients. Conversely, emphasizing the status gap, pointing up the
nonegalitarian quality of the relationship, and maintaining a social
distance from the patient might have a reverse effect. Expressing
overt hostility and aggression toward patients who are perceived as
disturbing the physician's professional role performance would tend
to maximize the status gap between the role partners.

Four items were posed to physicians and the wording ad-
justed appropriately for each of the ethnic groups of patients. These
were as follows:

a. Doctors tend to receive patients in different ways. Let us assume that a Moroccan (or Rumanian) patient has just come
   into your office and his record is before you. How do you
   generally start the conversation:
   1. Shalom, Mr. [patient's name]
   2. Shalom, Sir
   3. Shalom
   4. Yes . . . ?
   5. Other

b. Do you generally remember most of your Moroccan (or Rumanian) patients from one visit to the next?
   1. I remember their names as well as details of their illness.
   2. I remember mainly the details about their illness.
   3. It is hard for me to remember them without seeing their
      record.

c. Do you find that Moroccan (or Rumanian) patients cause
   difficulties and refuse to cooperate, so that you are forced to
   use authoritative measures with them?
   1. Very often

2. Occasionally
3. Hardly ever
4. Never

d. Some doctors say that the only way to work effectively with Moroccan (or Rumanian) patients is by maintaining a certain distance between a doctor and his patient. What is your attitude toward Moroccan (or Rumanian) patients who come to you for treatment?

1. I find it necessary to emphasize my status as a doctor.
2. I don't particularly emphasize my status as a doctor.
3. Just the opposite: I try to make them forget the status difference between us.

Our prediction was borne out. While only two of the four items show significant differences (questions b and c), they are all consistent in indicating more status-giving by physicians to Rumanian than to Moroccan clients. It is worth recalling that these data are drawn from physicians' reports of their behavior and not from direct observations of actual practice. In this case we might expect some deviance from reality in reporting since the subject dealt with is one that would be likely to induce external conformity to professional and societal norms, that is, according maximum status to clients. The differences which emerge in physicians' orientation to the two ethnic groups are therefore especially striking and we can surmise that actual differences on a behavioral level might be even greater.

These findings suggest a lack of congruence or complementarity between Kupat Holim physicians and certain of their patients, particularly the Moroccan group. We have seen on the one hand that the Moroccans are characterized by a comparatively high need for status—particularly the younger subgroups among them. Physicians, on the other hand, accord them relatively less of this type of reward. Whether this is due to the lesser conformity of Moroccan clients to expected patterns of patient behavior or to prejudice which has been internalized by physicians cannot be determined with certainty. But the lack of complementarity in the physician-patient relationship is fairly clear. It is worth noting in this context that, compared to Rumanians, Moroccans express themselves as somewhat less satisfied with Kupat Holim: 64 per cent of

the Moroccans report themselves satisfied with Kupat Holim services while 72 per cent of the Rumanians state this.

SUMMARY

   The status hypothesis has been confirmed in two clearly
defined subgroups: the less acculturated, more tradition-bound
Kurds and the Poles. This means that among these people, individuals with a high status need and a tendency to define themselves
as ill are likely to perceive the Kupat Holim clinic physician as
potentially satisfying their need for status. The socially mobile, more
Israel-oriented segments of the non-European groups fail to show
the predicted pattern. The Rumanians as a whole do not confirm
the hypothesis but we were unable to observe them in detail because of the small size of the critical group among them.

   Discussions with physicians as well as the more formal findings led us to think that we had originally exaggerated the level
of prestige and status of the Kupat Holim clinic physician; it seems
more reasonable to assume that his actual prestige may be lower
than we thought. Specialists and hospital doctors appear to rank
considerably higher within the profession than the general practitioner in the neighborhood clinic. Clients too quickly become aware
of this differentiated status. In that case those portions of the non-
European groups which are most aware of this would not confirm
the hypothesis, that is, they would not view the Kupat Holim physician as a potential source of gaining status through association or
contact. But the more traditional subgroups, which may be less
sensitive to shifts in physicians' status, continue to place him somewhat on a pedestal—and clients with the appropriate need for status and a high tendency to define themselves as ill are therefore
particularly likely to perceive the doctor as high in status. For the
latter type of client the need for status might be satisfied through
contact with the physician and the medical institution with which
he is associated.

   The hypothesis is also confirmed among the Polish respondents, but we have suggested on a post hoc level that the rationale
is apparently different because the generally high level of education
and occupational status of the Poles makes the interpretation suggested for the non-Europeans inappropriate. We have proposed that

the pattern may be explained by the high proportion of Polish physicians practicing within the Kupat Holim framework, or possibly in terms of certain cultural factors in the background of the Polish immigrants. Many of the Polish practitioners are veteran members of the Kupat Holim staff, having immigrated in large numbers before the establishment of the state. This results in their occupying a relatively large number of positions of prestige and power in the professional Kupat Holim structure. Polish patients would therefore tend to encounter a disproportionately large number of high status physicians of their own ethnic group and their image of the profession could be affected by this experience.

We do not find evidence that high frequency of clinic utilization is a function of clients' need for status. Observing that segment of the need-tendency group which perceives the Kupat Holim physician as high in status, that is, those who presumably see Kupat Holim as a potential locus for attaining status, does not show them to be especially frequent clinic attenders. Neither do we find them to be characterized by an especially high level of satisfaction with Kupat Holim and its services. Our conclusions must therefore be that clinic attendance does not appear to be a result of Kupat Holim clients' seeking to enjoy the status-giving latent function of the institution.

When we examined the opposite side of the coin, we found evidence for differential patterns of orientation of physicians toward clients of different ethnic origin. Less status is given by physicians to Moroccan than to Rumanian patients. We have suggested that this differentiation may be a function of the lesser conformity of Moroccan clients to the norms of expected patient behavior. It may also result from expressions of ethnic prejudice which are prevalent in Israeli society and which may have been internalized by physicians in their nonprofessional roles but which "spill over" into the professional context as well.

Client need and physician response do not complement each other in this case. The fact that physicians tend to give less status to Moroccans could be particularly disturbing to this group in light of its comparatively high need for rewards of this sort. Among them people with a need for status and a tendency to define themselves as ill do not perceive the Kupat Holim physician as particularly high in status. We have already pointed out that this group may have become aware of the lesser status position of the Kupat Holim clinic physician; another possibility is that they are more sensitive to the physician's differential orientation toward clients of different ethnic origin and particularly to his lesser willingness to accord them as much status as he does to clients of other ethnic origins. It would be our guess that such clients would attempt to seek elsewhere in the social system for contexts in which their need for status can be satisfied. But for them the Kupat Holim clinic physician has two strikes against him as a potential satisfier of their status need: his lowered status position in their eyes and his lesser willingness to accord them status.

10

Magic-Science Conflict

The cultural heterogeneity of the Israeli population is reflected in widely differing experiences with medical care before immigration and results in a positive orientation toward traditional, non-Western, medical practices and practitioners among some segments of the population. These orientations are often based on nonscientific, nonrational grounds and are legitimized by reference to tradition (King, 1962). They can be functional for illnesses for which Western medicine cannot provide unambiguous and efficacious remedies. Although traditional orientations might be concentrated more heavily among the non-European population, there could also be some Europeans characterized by such attitudes and orientations.

Our analysis assumes that the dominant Israeli value system tends to emphasize science, rationality, and empiricism and would therefore put a certain pressure on people adhering to traditional medical beliefs and practices. Except within the context of insulated reference groups, general opinion would be likely to disvalue such traditional practices. No matter how isolated their lives from the mainstream of Israeli society, it would probably be difficult for such people to escape the feeling that these attitudes are not quite up to the times. Such a situation of disequilibrium would put these people under pressure to seek some reconciliation of these values in an attempt to restore system-balance. Other mechanisms for coping with this sort of value conflict are for the individual to avoid contact with the wider social system by isolating himself within his traditional group, or to insulate the two value systems from each other in his everyday life, utilizing each in a specific, non-overlapping situation. These adaptive mechanisms are not too easily usable in the Israeli context. The concept of need as used in this chapter therefore refers to a need to restore equilibrium by resolution of value conflict. In our original model we included a variable which, it was thought, would filter out tradition-oriented people who are in conflict. This was attempted by asking whether certain salient reference groups agreed or disagreed with the respondent's orientation to traditional medical practice. Our assumption was that tradition-oriented respondents who reported that their families or salient reference groups disagreed with their orientation would be in greater conflict. This agreement-disagreement variable proved empirically to show a poor distribution: very few respondents reported such conflict. We therefore decided not to use it. This means that we infer a certain conflict among people with a positive orientation to traditional medical practice. As noted, such an inference is based on the assumption that the Israeli value context will exert certain pressures on such tradition-oriented respondents—and will generate the need as described.

The hypothesis which the present chapter seeks to test focuses on the Kupat Holim clinic as a potential institutional context for satisfying this need: by reducing discomfort and disequilibrium. This is accomplished through the availability of the Kupat Holim clinic as a context in which expression can be given to an exaggerated, positive attitude toward Western medicine and science. Such an orientation could provide clients characterized by traditional medical values with a means of assuaging the discomfort they feel because of their non-Western attitudes. The Kupat Holim clinic is one of the few easily accessible institutional contexts in which confidence in Western-oriented, scientific values can be demonstratively expressed.

It is worth noting that people can maintain a parallel set of orientations and in fact may be positively oriented both to traditional medical practitioners and to Kupat Holim clinic facilities. These are not mutually exclusive (King, 1962). This apparent paradox is resolved by such clients through an exaggerated confidence in the objectivity and scientific exactness of medicine, which can be thought of as a form of "magicism" that tradition-oriented people transfer to the medical context. Such hyperconfidence in Western medicine can therefore be viewed as consistent with a traditional approach to medical practitioners.

For these reasons our expectation is that tradition-oriented people will express extreme confidence in the objectivity and scientific exactness of the medical profession while the less tradition-oriented will be more aware of the limitations of Western medical practice and of the role intuition plays in it (compare Suchman, 1964). As in the other hypotheses, the tendency to define oneself as ill plays a filtering role so that our specific prediction focuses on the subgroup which is characterized both by a positive orientation toward traditional medical practice and by a high tendency to define itself as ill.

OVERVIEW OF VARIABLES

The definition of need used in this chapter is based on the assumption that a positive orientation to traditional medical practices and practitioners induces a certain value conflict and therefore a need to resolve the resulting disequilibrium. This need was defined in terms of respondents' confidence or belief in the usefulness of amulets or talismans in curing or preventing ailments and in the effectiveness of traditional medical practitioners, as contrasted to Western practitioners, in dealing with physical and mental illness.

The four ethnic groups differ from each other in their orientation to traditional medical practice. The Moroccans and Kurds show the most positive orientation, the Rumanians show a positive orientation somewhat less frequently, while the Poles are almost all nontraditional in their orientation. This order among the groups is about what we would expect in terms of general information about the cultural backgrounds of the ethnic groups chosen and it lends a certain validity to this variable (see Chapter Three).

A closer look at this patterning indicates that among the non-Europeans it is mostly the rural residents, female, and less educated segments of the population who are most characterized by a positive orientation to traditional medical practices and practitioners. Among the Rumanians it is mostly the less educated. This configuration indicates that positive attitudes toward traditional medical practitioners are concentrated most heavily among those portions of the population which are least socialized into Israeli society.

A set of questions was posed which attempted to measure respondents' feelings concerning the relative amounts of exactness and objectivity as contrasted to intuition and guesswork used by physicians within the framework of Western medicine. Most observers of the medical profession, as well as most physicians themselves, would probably agree that the professional role—even on its most competent level—is based on a certain measure of intuition and informed guessing in both diagnosis and treatment (Fletcher, 1963; Morris, 1964; Todd, 1953; Witts, 1964). Questions in this area were deliberately designed to permit expressions of excessive confidence in the ability of the physician to adhere exclusively to absolute objectivity and strictly rational criteria in his professional role. The specific questions therefore refer to the relative amount of guessing and intuition used by the doctor and to the possibility of completely objective interpretation of laboratory findings.

Our data show that the Moroccans and Kurds are more likely than the Europeans to express an exaggerated confidence in the objectivity and scientific exactness of the medical profession. The more detailed, controlled analysis of this variable again shows that those subgroups which are less acculturated into Israeli society are most likely to express an extremely high level of confidence in the scientific exactness of medicine and are less aware of the intuitive aspects of medical practice. This conclusion is based on the clear positive relationship of this variable to age in almost all of the ethnic groups.

The magic-science hypothesis is confirmed, but not very strongly (see Table 17). What Table 17 actually shows is that a positive orientation to traditional medical practices predisposes people to over-confidence in Western medicine; the tendency to define oneself as ill apparently plays only a minor role in this configuration. It will be recalled that the tendency variable was introduced as a means of filtering out those people who would be likely to seek out this particular institution, as an alternative to other possible institutional or situational contexts, to satisfy a specified need. In the case of the need generated by a positive orientation to traditional medical practice, the need focuses fairly specifically on a medical context so that it is reasonable to presume that Kupat Holim is almost the only context in which satisfaction can be obtained. Hence it would seem that the failure of the tendency variable to play the predicted role is easily explainable.

When we check the hypothesis within subgroups of the population we find that the above generalization requires further refinement. The only groups to provide fairly clear confirmation of the hypothesis are the older, non-Europeans; among the urban Moroccans and rural Kurds we also find women confirming the hypothesis. Our more specific conclusion must therefore be that the hypothesis is confirmed among those subgroups of the non-European population which are least acculturated into Israeli life.

These findings make necessary a certain revision in our thinking on the structure of the magic-science hypothesis. It will be recalled that our definition of need for this hypothesis is based on an assumption of value conflict—specifically focused on people with a positive orientation to traditional medical practice who, it was thought, would feel the pressures of a Western-oriented Israeli society and a consequent need to resolve such apparent conflict. But confirmation of the hypothesis appears specifically among those subgroups of the population which are least acculturated into Israeli society and would therefore be least likely to be aware of these pressures. Our original thinking would have led us to expect confirmation of the hypothesis among the relatively few younger, better educated, or less religious subgroups of the popula-

Table 17

CLIENTS' CONFIDENCE IN SCIENTIFIC OBJECTIVITY OF MEDICINE

Traditional Orientation, Tendency to Define Oneself as Ill	Clients' Perception of the Kupat Holim Physician (percentages):			
	Exclusive reliance on completely exact and objective criteria	Somewhat exact and somewhat intuitive	Frequent use of intuition and guessing	N
Traditional orientation, high tendency	62[a]	36	2	398
Traditional orientation, low tendency	58	39	3	277
Non-traditional orientation, high tendency	54	43	3	604
Non-traditional orientation, low tendency	50	46	4	551

[a] The difference between the critical group and all others combined (when the middle and right-hand column are also combined) is significant. $X^2 = 10.18$, D.F. $= 1$, $.01 > P > .001$.

tion who are still positively oriented to traditional medical practices. These would seem to be the subgroups most subject to the type of conflicting pressures we have described.

The findings therefore lead to a revision in our interpretation of this configuration. The fact that the hypothesis is confirmed among the least acculturated subgroups of the non-European population suggests a certain carry-over of magicism to perception of the Kupat Holim physician: the critical group, rather than seeking to resolve conflict, is apparently finding expression in this context for its general traditional orientation through hyperconfidence in the doctor, an attitude which can be viewed as a sort of magical orientation toward him. Excessive confidence in the scientific objectivity and rationality of medicine thus appears to be part of a total traditional-magical orientation among the less Western-oriented respondents rather than a mechanism to restore the disequilibrium brought about by a culture conflict.

Taking our analysis one step farther we have divided the four need-tendency groups in terms of the level of confidence expressed in the objectivity and scientific exactness of medicine. The resulting eight subgroups are then observed on a number of dimensions of general orientation to Kupat Holim: reported frequency of clinic attendance, satisfaction with clinic service, and extent of utilization of other medical facilities rather than those provided by Kupat Holim. Since the hypothesis has been confirmed, it seems reasonable to expect that the need-tendency group which satisfies its need—in this case expresses an extremely high level of confidence in the scientific exactness of medicine—should also be uniquely positive on the three variables measuring general orientation to Kupat Holim. Table 18 shows these findings.

Section A of Table 18 shows the utilization pattern— specifically, the frequency of clinic attendance. It is striking that the critical group shows comparatively high frequency of utilization and this occurs regardless of the level of confidence expressed in the Kupat Holim physician. There is no significant difference in the critical group between those characterized by "high confidence" and those characterized by "realistic doubts."

There is some reason to believe that the critical group is generally sicker and this sickness could account for these high

Table 18

UTILIZATION AND ATTITUDE PATTERNS TOWARD KUPAT HOLIM: MAGIC-SCIENCE HYPOTHESIS

Traditional Orientation, Tendency to Define Oneself as Ill	A. Percentage who report 20 or more visits a year to Kupat Holim doctor:[a] Perception of Kupat Holim doctor:[a] High confidence in absolute scientific ability of doctor	Realistic doubts about absolute scientific exactness of doctor	B. Percentage who report themselves satisfied with medical care of Kupat Holim[b] Perception of Kupat Holim doctor: High confidence in absolute scientific ability of doctor	Realistic doubts about absolute scientific exactness of doctor	C. Percentage who use only Kupat Holim, do not use private or other clinics Perception of Kupat Holim doctor: High confidence in absolute scientific ability of doctor	Realistic doubts about absolute scientific exactness of doctor
Traditional orientation, high tendency	24[c] (240)	33[d] (137)	72 (243)	54 (146)	89 (243)	74 (144)
Traditional orientation, low tendency	8 (154)	13 (111)	71 (158)	55 (112)	80 (157)	68 (108)
Non-traditional orientation, high tendency	19 (324)	13 (268)	68 (323)	68 (274)	83 (316)	75 (265)
Non-traditional orientation, low tendency	8 (271)	9 (271)	66 (263)	58 (269)	78 (271)	69 (263)

[a] In order to assure a sufficient number of cases the scale defining confidence in the objectivity and scientific exactness of medicine was dichotomized and not trichotomized as in Table 14.

[b] See Footnote a to Table 8.

[c] The difference between the critical group and the three others combined (among those with high confidence) is significant: $X^2 = 16.44$, D.F. $= 1$, $P < .001$.

[d] The difference between the critical group and the three others combined (among those with realistic doubts) is significant: $X^2 = 44.11$, D.F. $= 1$, $P < .001$.

utilization rates. In an attempt to check this we have observed frequency of clinic utilization among sick and healthy respondents: the pattern already noted is confirmed clearly in the self-defined healthy group. See Table 19. While the critical group among the sick also shows comparatively high clinic attendance, an equally frequent attendance pattern is shown in the group characterized by a nontraditional orientation and a high tendency to define themselves as ill.

It therefore seems appropriate to conclude that people characterized by a positive orientation to traditional medical practices and a tendency to define themselves as ill visit the physician with comparatively high frequency. This finding parallels our conclusion on the hypotheses concerning catharsis and coping with failure where we also found that the need-tendency typology effectively predicts frequency of clinic utilization. In all three cases, the latent function appears to be attracting clinic attendance and could be contributing to high utilization rates.

In contrast to the findings on frequency of clinic attendance, we do not find the critical group showing unique behavior or attitudes with respect to the other two variables observed in Table 18. Sections B and C of this table indicate that members of the critical group are generally similar to the remainder of the population in expressing satisfaction with Kupat Holim or in using its facilities exclusively. Thus, in terms of the three dimensions of general orientation to Kupat Holim, only the frequency of clinic attendance shows the critical group to indicate unique behavior.

However, it is worth noting in sections B and C of Table 18 that people with high confidence in the absolute scientific ability of the doctor show a higher level of general satisfaction with Kupat Holim and generally tend to more exclusive use of its facilities. Those characterized by realistic doubts are somewhat more prone to use other medical facilities.

Physicians' Response. Many physicians find it easier to carry out their professional role if they accept uncritically some patients' tendency to attribute a higher level of scientific accuracy and objectivity to them than they themselves believe to characterize their professional work. Patients who are completely confident and do not question medical procedures are often easier to deal with.

Table 19

FREQUENCY OF VISITS TO DOCTOR AMONG "SICK" AND "HEALTHY" RESPONDENTS: MAGIC-SCIENCE HYPOTHESIS

Traditional Orientation, Tendency to Define Oneself as Ill	Percentage who report 20 or more visits a year to Kupat Holim doctor among self-defined sick respondents[a],[b]		Percentage who report 10 or more visits a year to Kupat Holim doctor among self-defined healthy respondents[a],[c]	
Traditional orientation, high tendency	38	(216)	28	(158)
Traditional orientation, low tendency	19	(91)	17	(173)
Non-traditional orientation, high tendency	38	(216)	12	(376)
Non-traditional orientation, low tendency	24	(145)	10	(398)

[a] We have used different cut-off points on frequency of visits to doctor for "sick" and "healthy" respondents. For the "sick," 20 or more visits per year were defined as high utilization, while for the "healthy," a frequency of 10 or more visits a year were considered high utilization.

[b] Respondents were defined as "sick" on the basis of this question: "Do you generally consider yourself a sick or a healthy person?" Persons who replied "Yes, very sick," or "Yes, fairly sick," or "somewhat sick," were categorized as "sick."

[c] Respondents who replied "fairly healthy" or "very healthy" were categorized as "healthy."

These qualities would seem to be typical of patients characterized by hyperconfidence in the scientific accuracy of the medical profession. The doctor, for his part, will be under pressure to play along with this attitude even if his professional conscience does not entirely condone it. This ambivalence could therefore result in some measure of discomfort on his part.

The alternative possibility to such uncritical acceptance is for the physician to enlighten these patients by stressing the tentativeness and necessary guesswork that go into many aspects of medical practice. While such enlightenment may serve to protect the physician from exaggerated hopes for the success of medical treatment and disappointment when it fails, it also makes his day-to-day professional tasks more difficult precisely because of the lower level of confidence and greater criticism such enlightenment is likely to produce. Thus there are rewards and costs in either of the alternatives he chooses.

The first of the two alternatives, that is, accepting without question the hyperconfidence of some patients, serves to satisfy patients' need as we have defined it in this chapter. Acceptance by the physician of such attitudes uncritically would permit patients to gain whatever satisfaction they can for this need through this mechanism; enlightening them with respect to the scientific limitations of medical practice tends to prevent satisfaction of the need in the Kupat Holim context. The logic of such need satisfaction is that if the patient needs the doctor to appear as a powerful, objective, semi-magical figure, the latter will fulfill this need most by adhering to this image.

In a broader context it may be suggested that the second of the two alternatives is more a socializing one: it enlightens the patient with respect to the limitations of medical practice and in this sense orients him more realistically to the situation. Furthermore, it attempts to prevent the transference of traditional patterns of orientation to a Western-geared medical system. In this sense it not only helps to socialize him into a modern medical subsystem but into the wider social system of Western-oriented Israeli society. In an immigrant society the physician may play a major role as such a socializing agent (Morag, 1966).

At the same time many physicians may not perceive their

professional role so broadly as to include the task or the obligation to socialize patients. They may feel that this job belongs to other professionals. And in fact undertaking this task undoubtedly requires an additional investment of time and effort. Particularly in a system such as Kupat Holim, in which the doctor is already under considerable pressure in terms of patient-load and bureaucratic obligations, he may be unable or unwilling to add this task to his already overburdened professional life. Thus it is possible for the physician ideologically to accept the task of socializing patients but to be unable, because of situational factors, to carry out the professional role as broadly as he might prefer. In such cases he may satisfy the need by default; that is, by failing to enlighten patients, he tends to accept hyperconfidence and "magicism" in their orientation.

The following introductory statement was presented to all physician respondents:

Some Moroccan (or Rumanian) patients continue to use traditional medical practices and practitioners for certain types of ailments. When such patients come to the Kupat Holim clinic they often tend to display exaggerated confidence in the physician's ability to cure and may even attribute semi-magical powers to him.

a. Would you say that Moroccan (or Rumanian) patients who attribute semi-magical powers to you disturb or annoy you in your practice?
    1. They disturb me very much.
    2. Disturb me a little.
    3. They don't disturb me very much.
    4. They don't disturb me at all.
b. Do you generally explain the limitations of the medical profession to this type of Moroccan (or Rumanian) patient, or do you feel that it's better for them to have excessive confidence in you and in your ability to cure?
    1. I always try to explain the limitations of the profession.
    2. I sometimes explain the limitations of the profession.
    3. I generally ignore this attitude of patients.
    4. I think it desirable for them to continue with this excessive confidence in medicine.

c. Do you find that excessive confidence in you and in your ability to cure helps in treating Moroccan (or Rumanian) patients?

    1. It hampers their treatment very much.
    2. It hampers their treatment somewhat.
    3. It helps their treatment somewhat.
    4. It helps their treatment very much.

The first of the three questions focuses on the affective component in physicians' response patterns. Table 20 (Section A) shows that physicians respond differently on this dimension to the two ethnic groups of patients: they state that they are more disturbed by Moroccan than by Rumanian patients who attribute semi-magical qualities to them. Forty-eight per cent report being disturbed by such attitudes of Moroccan patients, while only 36 per cent are disturbed by Rumanian patients showing such hyperconfidence. We already know that Moroccans in fact display such behavior with greater frequency than Rumanians. It is feasible that this lower level of tolerance for Moroccans is a result of the greater prevalence of the phenomenon among members of this group such that physicians' threshold of tolerance has, in a sense, been passed. On the other hand it is possible that this attitude is part of a generally lower level of tolerance for many types of behavior of Moroccan patients.

In the course of the group discussions several physicians spoke with some condescension of "ignorant" patients: "We have many primitive patients who don't know how to behave. When I give them suppositories, they swallow them." "The trouble is that our patients are ignorant and uncultured." "They have no education, they push each other around. They can't explain what their symptoms are."

Occasionally there was a specific reference to Moroccans or Kurds: "Immigrants from North Africa are ignorant and lack culture. Whatever I do for them, they don't understand." "Patients from Kurdistan and Morocco who never saw a doctor before in their lives come to the clinic practically every day and some days they come several times."

Section B of Table 20, which explores what physicians are likely to do when they encounter such attitudes, shows that they are more likely to accept such behavior on the part of Moroccan patients but to make a greater effort to enlighten Rumanian patients when they display these patterns of hyperconfidence. This is seen by the fact that 28 per cent of the physicians "always try to explain the limitations of the profession" to Rumanian patients, while only 19 per cent make this effort with their Moroccan patients. Furthermore, 37 per cent of the physicians believe that such hyperconfidence should be ignored or is desirable among Moroccan patients while only 25 per cent state this with respect to their Rumanian patients.

The data indicate that physicians differ in their pattern of orientation to patients, in some cases following a policy of enlightenment and in others letting well enough alone. We are unable to determine in detail what factors determine just which policy will be followed, but the differential orientation toward the two ethnic groups is suggestive. Physicians may feel that it is more worthwhile or productive to attempt to enlighten their Rumanian patients because Moroccans, with their generally lower level of education, may appear less amenable to such a policy. Furthermore, the greater frequency of this pattern of hyperconfidence among Moroccans could cause physicians to feel that the pattern is normative and deeply rooted among them so that enlightenment would be less likely to work effectively. Stereotyped perceptions of the two ethnic groups could result in physicians feeling that Rumanian patients should know better than to show such patterns while Moroccans can be accepted in a less enlightened role.

Section C of Table 20 refers to the physician's feelings concerning implications of patient's hyperconfidence for his actual ability to carry out his professional role effectively. About a fifth of the physicians feel that hyperconfidence impedes their role performance and approximately a third state that it in fact helps them, but there are no differences with respect to the two ethnic groups of patients. On this dimension, in contrast to the two others, physicians seem to be characterized by a similar orientation to Rumanian and Moroccan patients.

It will be recalled that a lack of differentiation in orientation to the two ethnic groups was also found in physicians' response to patients' need for catharsis and some aspects of coping with

Table 20

PHYSICIANS' RESPONSE TO PATIENTS' HYPERCONFIDENCE
IN MEDICINE

A. "Would you say that Moroccan (or Rumanian) patients who attribute semi-magical powers to you disturb or annoy you in your practice?"

Patient Group	Very much or somewhat	Not much	Not at all	N
Rumanians	36	40	24	217
Moroccans	48	39	13	114

$X^2 = 7.03$, D.F. $= 2$, $.05 > P > .02$.

B. "Do you generally explain the limitations of the medical profession to this type of Moroccan (or Rumanian) patient, or do you feel that it's better for them to have excessive confidence in you and in your ability to cure?"

	Ignore or think it desirable	Sometimes explain	Always try to explain	N
Rumanians	25	47	28	220
Moroccans	37	44	19	111

$X^2 = 6.55$, D.F. $= 2$, $.05 > P > .02$.

C. "Do you find that excessive confidence in you and in your ability to cure among Moroccan (or Rumanian) patients helps in treating them?"

	Yes, helps very much	Helps somewhat	No, hampers somewhat or very much	N
Rumanians	32	50	18	216
Moroccans	40	40	20	114

$X^2 = 2.64$, D.F. $= 2$, $.30 > P > .20$.

failure. Our interpretation there was based on the closeness of those variables to the manifest functions of medical practice and the universalistic norms which presumably pervade it. The question being considered here includes a similar component: it refers to the relevance of patients' level of confidence in the physician's ability to treat Moroccan and Rumanian patients. In contrast to the other two questions posed in this area, this question focuses specifically on the quality of medical care dispensed. Such a formulation could well cause physicians to verbalize their response in terms of the universalistic norms of the profession which prescribe equal treatment to all.

Checking the conclusions drawn from Table 20 among subgroups of physicians shows no significant differences among men and women doctors, age groups, or physicians with differing seniority in the profession. We do find, however, that physicians who have themselves immigrated more recently show a somewhat greater tendency to socialize patients by trying to enlighten them by explaining the realistic limitations of the medical profession. Old-timers in Israel are more likely to let well enough alone or to believe that excessive confidence in medicine may actually be a good thing. This finding taken with the absence of any relationship to physicians' age or seniority in the profession suggests that it may be the experience of practice in Israel, itself, which causes physicians to lose some of their enthusiasm for education of the patient. It is not impossible that such experience might lead physicians to the conclusion that it is not possible or fruitful to try to enlighten patients.

There is no explicit recognition in the doctors' discussion of the problem of overconfidence by patients or of the need to enlighten patients on this subject. On the other hand, there is some reference to the physician's more general role as educator, although it was not feasible to check whether this role is more commonly taken by newly arrived physicians. "Patients need lots of explanations. We've got to help them understand what we're all up against." "When I see that a patient doesn't understand, I explain to him a second time. This is what needs to be done." "We have to educate these people. Whatever I have achieved during my years of practice has been through my own program of educating patients." "Patients must be taught discipline. And if they come from poor backgrounds, we have to teach them."

SUMMARY

The non-European groups under observation show a more frequent positive orientation to traditional medical practices and practitioners than the European groups. They are also more likely to express high confidence in the absolute objectivity and exactness of medical science and to be less aware than the Europeans of the limitations of the profession or the guesswork that goes into a considerable measure of medical diagnosis and therapy. Both of these qualities appear in an even more concentrated form among those subgroups of the non-Europeans which are less socialized into Israeli society: women, older people, the less educated.

The hypothesis is confirmed among the more traditional subgroups of the non-Europeans. We may therefore conclude that the latent function occurs but possibly for different reasons than we originally proposed. It was first thought that the need to resolve the conflict generated by the confrontation of a positive orientation to traditional medical practice with the Western values of Israeli society would express itself in a pattern of hyperconfidence in Western medicine: such conflict should be most strongly felt, it would seem, by younger, better educated people who are also characterized by a positive orientation to traditional medical practice. These are the more socialized subgroups which still adhere to traditional medical beliefs. In fact, the opposite is the case: it is precisely the less socialized and less Westernized subgroups which have confirmed the hypothesis by showing a high level of confidence in the scientific exactness and objectivity of modern medicine. We have therefore suggested that this pattern may be conditioned less by the need for conflict resolution than by a tendency to transfer the "magicism" characteristic of traditional medical beliefs to a modern, Western-oriented setting.

In addition, we find that people characterized by a positive orientation to traditional medical practice and by a high tendency to define themselves as ill are unusually frequent utilizers of the Kupat Holim clinic: they report more visits to see the physician than the remainder of the population. It therefore appears that clients may be seeking out the institution in order to enjoy this latent function.

When we consider physicians' response to these patterns of belief of their patients, we find a differentiated pattern in doctors' attitudes toward patients of different ethnic backgrounds. Less tolerance and greater annoyance are felt by physicians toward Moroccan that toward Rumanian patients expressing a positive orientation to traditional medical practices. We have suggested that this differential attitude may be a function of the greater frequency of traditional medical beliefs among Moroccan patients or of a lower level of general tolerance for Moroccans. Physicians also report making more of an effort at enlightening Rumanian than Moroccan patients on the realistic limitations of medical practice and the guesswork that inevitably goes into it. Taking the two findings together, we may conclude that physicians are less tolerant of traditional medical beliefs of Moroccan patients but also less willing to socialize them into the realities of Western medical practice. Although there seems to be some awareness among the doctors of their general role as educators, there is no explicit reference to this particular type of socialization. This pattern serves in a sense to satisfy the comparatively greater need of Moroccan patients for a locus in which they can express the "magicism" characteristic of their traditional beliefs. At the same time it carries at least two negative implications: it may communicate a measure of intolerance or hostility to Moroccan patients and it may also slow down the general process of acculturation into Israeli society.

PART FOUR

CLOSING

11

Social Functions of
Medical Practice

We have considered each of the five latent functions separately in an attempt to shed some light on the role each plays. What conclusions may we now draw concerning the medical institution and its social functions? How do the separate sets of findings fit together to answer the more general questions initially posed? In an attempt to elucidate these questions we draw our findings together in a summary that recapitulates the rationale of the research strategy and cross-cuts the various topics dealt with separately thus far.

It will be recalled that our basic approach to the study of latent functions has been in terms of the institution's potential for satisfying certain needs of clients. The concern with latent rather than manifest functions has necessarily resulted in a focus on non-medical needs. When the institution can be said to be satisfying such needs, we conclude that a latent function is being activated.

Five needs were considered: need for catharsis, coping with failure, status, integration into Israeli society, and resolution of a magic-science conflict. These needs are associated with the immigration process but are not confined to immigrants: we may assume that people with such needs exist in many societies although with different frequencies. It is in this sense that the present study has generality well beyond the Israeli situation in which it was carried out. The particular locus of the study serves to highlight populations which are characterized by a high frequency of certain of these needs.

The basic paradigm of the analysis is built on a combination of each need with a variable called the tendency to define oneself as ill. The latter was introduced in an attempt to filter out clients who would be likely to seek out the medical institution, rather than other social contexts, to satisfy their need. The analysis focuses on the subgroup of the population characterized by a high need and a high tendency which is predicted to be more likely than others to satisfy the need through the institution and to be characterized by high frequency of clinic utilization.

Four immigrant groups of Jews from Kurdistan, Morocco, Rumania, and Poland were included, the first three in both urban and rural communities. These ethnic groups were chosen because they differ in the extent of traditionalism of their basic social patterns and values and in the extent of their experience with Western medicine. Much of the analysis is concerned with comparisons of these ethnic groups.

The point of view of the client has been taken as central in determining the nature of the latent functions. While other points of view might also be taken as a point of departure—for example, those expressed by Kupat Holim personnel or by official spokesmen of the institution—we have chosen to focus on clients as the principal recipients of Kupat Holim services. It would seem that their point of view on this issue is crucial: the latent functions exist to the extent that *they*—and not other representatives of the institution —feel them (Levy, 1952). Physicians may claim, for example, that they permit all patients to talk freely, thus satisfying their need for catharsis. But physicians could be operating under an illusion that they satisfy the need when in fact they do not. They may, consciously or unconsciously, be satisfying it differentially for various subgroups of patients. Unless patients who need such supportive listening report empirically that they obtain it from the Kupat Holim physician, we cannot conclude that the institution is characterized by this latent function.

The nature of the needs considered made it somewhat difficult to measure the extent of their satisfaction by means of questions posed directly to Kupat Holim members. In considering the classic case of the latent functions of a political party, Merton (1949) would be able to ask directly whether an individual or his family received a food basket within a specified time period; it is much more problematic to ask a Kupat Holim member whether he gained status through his contacts with the medical institution, whether it assisted him in becoming integrated into the social system, or whether the institution aided him in coping with feelings of failure. Since we are committed to the principle of basing our conclusions on data obtained directly from Kupat Holim members, a variety of tactics was devised to select variables that would tell us something of clients' feelings of need satisfaction through the medical institution or its personnel. Some of these measures proved more successful than others and we are not entirely satisfied with all of them. In considering future research possibilities, it would seem that effort could profitably be directed toward a sharpening of some of those measures.

Chapter Four provides empirical evidence that clinic utilization rates in Kupat Holim are among the highest in the world. This high utilization is especially concentrated among the less acculturated immigrants who have not yet moved into the mainstream of Israeli society.

An attempt has been made to help explain these high utilization rates by clients' desire and need to enjoy the latent functions of the medical institution. We have asked whether clients may be attending the clinic in an attempt to gain certain rewards over and above the manifest ones of therapy or prevention of illness. The analysis presented may therefore be said to focus on two related questions: (1) Is the medical institution characterized by the latent functions? and (2) Can the latent functions—if they exist—help explain high clinic utilization rates?

The clearest confirmation of our expectations occurs when the answer to both of these questions is affirmative. This happens when clients' feelings point to the existence of the latent function *and* high utilization rates appear to be associated with it. However, it is also feasible for the latent function to exist in the eyes of the institution's clients but it may not be associated with particularly high frequency of clinic utilization. In contrast there may be evidence that clients are frequent clinic attenders but do not seem to be seeking out the latent functions. Finally it is possible that the answers to both of these questions are negative.

This research has not attempted to explore other factors which could be causing high clinic utilization. The focus has been almost exclusively on a specific set of clients' needs. Additional research is needed to determine how the patterns found here relate to other structural factors in the medical system which could be contributing to high frequency of physician utilization. We refer to certain dysfunctional aspects of the medical bureaucracy which put pressure on physicians to receive a certain number of patients each hour, thus preventing them in many cases from dispensing adequate medical care: one mechanism to solve this problem is for the doctor to request the patient to return again and again. Similarly, decision-making in such medical structures is often held up through sending patients from specialist to specialist, from laboratory to laboratory. Such practices increase utilization rates and delay or possibly even avoid the need for decision-making. Exploration of these problems and their relationship to the latent functions requires a rather different research strategy than the one used in our undertaking.

LATENT FUNCTIONS

The most striking set of evidence concerns two of the latent functions in which clients' perception patterns as well as their behavior in terms of clinic utilization rates confirm our expectations: provision of a setting for catharsis and resolution of a magic-science conflict.

Kupat Holim members characterized by a high need for catharsis and a tendency to define themselves as ill report that they obtain satisfaction of this need from the clinic physician. By our definition, catharsis-giving is therefore a latent function of the medical institution. While the empirical finding is not striking statistically, it is significant and sufficient to permit us to conclude that the institution performs this function for clients with this need. Improvement of the instrument used might sharpen the findings.

What is more, people characterized by a high need for catharsis and a tendency to define themselves as ill are also frequent clinic utilizers. Such high utilization appears among people with a high need for catharsis regardless of whether they succeed or fail in satisfying that need through the clinic physician. Enjoyment of the latent function apparently occurs among those who report that the Kupat Holim physician satisfies their need for catharsis. On the other hand, it is somewhat puzzling that those with a need for catharsis who do not obtain satisfaction through the Kupat Holim physician also show a high frequency of clinic utilization. We have characterized such people as manifesting a ritual pattern, that is, people who continue attending the clinic frequently in a persistent and undiscouraged hope of gaining satisfaction at some future date.

In sum, these findings provide affirmative answers to both questions posed: catharsis-giving is a latent function of the medical institution and it apparently motivates some clients to utilize the clinic in an effort to gain satisfaction for the need.

The Kurds, who are the most traditional group included in the study, reveal a striking pattern with respect to the catharsis-giving function of the medical institution. Kurdish immigrants with a need for catharsis obtain satisfaction of this need through their contacts with the physician *and* with the clinic nurse. The latter plays a role complementary to that of the physician with respect to catharsis-giving—specifically for this most traditional group. Furthermore, as noted, their need for catharsis is associated with an especially high frequency of clinic attendance. Such a double pattern leads to the conclusion that the catharsis-giving function may be particularly salient to the most traditional ethnic groups.

An equally clear pattern appears with respect to the latent function concerning resolution of a magic-science conflict, but only among the most traditional subgroups of the non-European immigrants. For them the institution seems to provide a locus to which they are able to transfer some of the "magicism" which characterizes traditional approaches to medicine. It is precisely those individuals among them who are characterized by the most traditional attitudes who also express hyperconfidence in the scientific objectivity and rationality of the Kupat Holim physician. It is no paradox to say that the medical institution fills a real need for them by providing an acceptable and legitimate locus for such "magical" attitudes to be expressed. Confidence or even overconfidence in medicine are normative in Western society so that expressions of such attitudes could reduce the feeling of backwardness of people who continue to adhere to traditional medical beliefs and practices. In this sense the medical institution satisfies a need and provides a rather special type of latent function.

Complementing this pattern, we find comparatively high frequency of clinic utilization among people characterized by a traditional orientation and a high tendency to define themselves as ill. We have taken this to mean that such people may be seeking out the latent function of the institution: they attend frequently at least partly in order to be able to express their attitudes of high confidence in the institution. If this is correct, then this latent function may also help explain high utilization rates, especially among traditional groups. As in the case of the catharsis-giving latent function, the answers to both of the questions posed are positive: a latent function concerning resolution of a magic-science conflict exists and it may help explain high clinic utilization rates.

The evidence on the latent function concerning coping with failure is less dramatic than the two summarized thus far but is nevertheless strongly suggestive. Clients report behavioral data which indicate that a feeling of failure coupled with the tendency to define oneself as ill is associated with high frequency of clinic attendance. In terms of clients' perception of the institution, however, our prediction is not borne out. Definition of the perception variable proved to be particularly tricky in this case and it is feasible that we may have shot wide of the mark in using clients' attitude toward the importance of sickness certificates as the perception variable. In a sense, satisfaction of the need to cope with failure is gained through clinic attendance per se—since this is the direct mechanism to gain legitimation from the physician for illness. If we take this point of view, we may argue that the findings do demonstrate the existence of the latent function—because people with a need, that is, those who feel failure, attend the clinic with high frequency presumably in an attempt to cope with such failure through illness.

The three latent functions discussed thus far help explain high clinic utilization rates. This means that need for catharsis, orientation to traditional medical practices, and feelings of failure are each positively correlated with clinic utilization. We have checked these findings for independence and have found that a simultaneous analysis of all three needs shows each of them to condition clinic utilization independently.

The two remaining latent functions—status-giving and integration into Israeli society—appear to operate for certain subgroups of the population but do not motivate high frequency of clinic attendance and cannot be thought relevant to the high rates of utilization characterizing Kupat Holim. In other words, the first of the two questions posed is answered positively, in part, but the second negatively.

In the case of the status-giving latent function, we find that the institution seems to satisfy a need for status in two rather different groups: the less acculturated, more traditional subgroup of the Kurds who are the most traditional group included in the study and the urban Poles. Our post hoc explanation is different for these two groups.

With respect to the first we noted that the status position of the Kupat Holim clinic physician is apparently lower than we had originally thought when we proposed the status hypothesis. As the research progressed and in the course of our contacts with clinic doctors, we gained the impression that the high status physicians are mostly the specialists and those practicing within a hospital framework; the general practitioner in the Kupat Holim clinic appears to rank somewhat lower in the internal professional hierarchy of the Israeli medical profession. If this is correct, our original formulation of the status hypothesis is not entirely appropriate since it is based on the assumption that the clinic physician occupies a higher status position than he apparently does. What is most interesting is the finding that this hypothesis is confirmed in the subgroup in which the status gap between their own position and that of the physician is comparatively large, that is, the less acculturated subgroup of the most traditional ethnic group. They apparently perceive the clinic physician to be markedly high in status and those among them with a high need for status and a tendency to define themselves as ill tend to gain satisfaction of this need through contact with him. We have therefore concluded that for them the latent function exists. However those segments of the population which are aware of the lowered status position of the Kupat Holim general practitioner do not perceive the institution as satisfying this need.

The urban Poles also seem to gain satisfaction of their need for status through contact with the Kupat Holim physician. The explanation proposed above is inappropriate for them because they are the most highly educated and occupationally skilled of all the groups included in the study. We have noted, however, that a disproportionately large number of Kupat Holim physicians tend themselves to be of Polish origin; these doctors have considerable seniority in the medical organization and probably occupy high status positions within it. We have suggested that Polish clients' image of the Kupat Holim physician might be affected by this pattern. As a result of contact with or knowledge of such Polish doctors, they might tend, more than others, to attribute high status to Kupat Holim practitioners. Another possibility could be associated with attitudinal patterns brought by these immigrants from their country of origin. We have been unable to separate out these possibilities but in both cases, as noted, they are post hoc explanations. What appears to be important is the fact that the Polish immigrants observed do tend to satisfy their need for status through contact with the Kupat Holim physician. We are therefore able to conclude that for them this latent function is operating.

A parallel pattern occurs with respect to the latent function relating to integration. Our prediction for this latent function focused on the Moroccan and Kurdish groups only and did not apply to the two European groups. This prediction is confirmed in terms of the perception patterns of the Moroccans and Kurds: in both groups people with a need for integration appear to obtain a certain satisfaction for that need through the medical institution. We may therefore conclude that for them the latent function is operating.

As noted, the operation of these last two latent functions—status-giving and integration into Israeli society—does not involve behavioral consequences in the form of high clinic utilization. The evidence does not indicate that people who gain satisfaction of these needs through the institution are especially high clinic attenders. The satisfaction obtained in the course of "normal" frequency of clinic attendance seems to be sufficient and clients are not motivated to visit their doctor more frequently in an attempt to enjoy the latent function even more.

Another possible interpretation of this pattern relates to the intensity of need and need satisfaction by the institution. Although we have focused on clients with a high level of need for status and for integration, our definitions of necessity are relative ones: clients with a high need are *higher than others* but may not be very high on an absolute level. The same is true of the institution's satisfaction of the need: the need-tendency group obtains more satisfaction *than others,* but on an absolute level this amount of satisfaction could be small. This suggests that the entire process may be operating at a low level of intensity. If this is the case it is understandable that clients would not be particularly motivated to attend the clinic more frequently in order to gain additional satisfaction for these needs. Our data do not permit systematic examination of this possibility.

We may summarize these findings as follows:

1. Catharsis-giving and resolution of a magic-science conflict are latent functions of the medical institution. A desire to enjoy them probably motivates certain groups to seek them out by means of frequent clinic attendance.

2. A need to cope with failure seems to motivate certain clients to attend the clinic frequently. Although the evidence concerning perception of the institution is unclear, we may reasonably suggest that the latent function of helping people cope with failure does characterize the institution.

3. The institution is characterized by latent functions of sta-

tus-giving and assistance in integration into Israeli society for some groups. But these latent functions apparently do not motivate clients to utilize the clinic with high frequency.

However, it is of some interest to note that our predictions with respect to patterns of perception of the institution have generally been confirmed only among the less Westernized, more traditional segments of the populations observed. With the exception of the Poles, who confirm the status hypothesis, we do not find that our hypotheses have been confirmed among the more westernized clients.

LATENT FUNCTIONS AND CLINIC UTILIZATION

As noted, Israel is characterized by unusually high clinic utilization rates. This has been established on the basis of a systematic comparison of Kupat Holim with comparable institutions in other countries. Nor does it appear that these rates are fully explained by the level of health of the Israeli population. This research has demonstrated that there is an association between immigration and clinic utilization: high frequency of utilization is concentrated among those segments of the population which have not yet entered fully into the mainstream of Israeli life. The sick role apparently serves as a mechanism to aid immigrants in the process of adjustment to a new social system. What is more, there is evidence that utilization rates fall off with time, presumably as immigrants assume the new social roles required of them and as they adapt to the social system. While it is possible that newly arrived immigrants are sicker and their level of health might improve with time, this research strongly suggests that certain social and psychological needs may also be motivating entry into the sick role as well as clinic attendance.

This pattern suggests that the medical institution fulfills an early socializing role for new immigrants, satisfying certain of their needs so that with time they no longer require the institution as much. It assumes that the relevant needs are reduced with time. Another explanation of the decline in utilization rates is that newly arrived immigrants are characterized by high expectations that the easily accessible and available medical institution will satisfy certain of their needs; with time they learn that it does not always perform this function in accordance with their expectations and so they begin to seek other institutional or personal contexts to obtain such need satisfaction. This approach does not assume that needs are reduced with time but that satisfaction is gradually sought elsewhere.

The nature of the immigrant populations included in the study made it difficult to determine precisely whether the level of various needs changes over time. This is because each group arrived in the country within a relatively brief time span. However there are some suggestive findings to shed light on this question. It would seem that the need to resolve a magic-science conflict, as we have defined it, appears less frequently in the population over time: younger, more educated segments of the population are less frequently characterized by a traditional orientation and there would therefore seem to be reason to believe that this need becomes less widespread in the population over time. Since we have shown that high clinic utilization is at least partly a result of clients' seeking to satisfy this need through clinic attendance, we may guess that this pattern will be less prominent in the future.

The findings presented here do not provide a basis to assume that the need for catharsis or feelings of failure are reduced with time. We have pointed out that there is reason to believe that clients with these needs are seeking satisfaction for them through clinic attendance. It may well be that such needs exist in many populations, and, while they may be associated with immigration, they are not limited only to immigrants. Immigration may intensify such needs, but there are other factors in the social system which could also cause them to appear. Additional population groups need to be studied before a systematic answer to this problem can be provided, but it is our feeling that the latent functions of assisting people to cope with failure and providing an appropriate setting for catharsis might have considerable generality and stability over time even in situations outside Israel.

The above would be true on condition that the clinic physician does not change his role radically with time. We have noted that the bureaucratic structure often places pressure on the physician and makes difficult appropriate role performance. One type of pressure focuses on the amount of time he is able to spend with patients, thus affecting directly his ability to provide an appropriate setting to satisfy the need for catharsis. Other bureaucratic conditions affect other aspects of his role performance. With the increasing size of medical institutions and growth of the populations using them, such bureaucratic pressures are also likely to grow and it seems reasonable to wonder whether the clinic practitioner will be able to maintain his traditional professional role structure. Certain changes might occur in this role with time. Once clients learn that the clinic physician no longer provides an appropriate setting for catharsis, they may begin to seek other contexts to satisfy this need.

It is our guess that the latent function of helping people cope with failure is the most stable of the latent functions discussed. It seems likely to persist in the face of possible changes in the structure of the professional role, and, as already noted, it probably has a good deal of generality to situations outside Israel. This is because of the special relationship of illness and failure, specifically the use of the former to rationalize and justify the latter. It seems unlikely that an equally convenient and attractive social mechanism will be developed to substitute for this. While a more affluent society might find less need to utilize illness as a criterion for allocation of rewards, this would only tend to reduce the frequency of need for this latent function: it would not eliminate it, because all societies, including the most affluent, have people characterized by feelings of failure, who will want to enjoy this latent function.

PHYSICIANS' RESPONSE

Doctors' response to clients was measured by means of a questionnaire in which they reported their own patterns of behavior in a clinic situation. While this method has the disadvantages of possible distortions in the direction of conformity to normative patterns, it is striking that physicians openly stated that their orientations to two ethnic groups of clients were not identical. Doctors' response patterns to Moroccan and Rumanian patients differ considerably with respect to several of the needs.

When clients' need is viewed by physicians as associated directly or indirectly with the manifest functions of the medical institution, they tend to state that their response to Moroccan and

Rumanian patients is similar. Such a pattern appears with respect to their willingness to allow patients to talk freely even when they stray from strictly medical subjects, that is, response to the need for catharsis. It also appears in their reports of medical treatment given to patients who may be sick as a result of failure. Indeed, many physicians consider unhampered listening to patients a necessary part of diagnosis. If this is the case, universalistic medical norms could be directing physicians' reports of their response to these needs of the two ethnic groups. Whether their actual behavior is correlated with these reports is another matter that cannot be directly ascertained by this research. One might surmise, however, that there is a greater likelihood of corresponding behavioral consequences if equality of response is claimed than if it is not even claimed.

But when the direct medical relevance of their behavior is less evident, we find physicians reporting that they respond differently to the two ethnic groups. The difference consistently expresses itself in greater sympathy, understanding, and tolerance for Rumanians as compared to Moroccan patients. Such differential orientations appear with respect to physicians' status-giving behavior, response to patients' overconfidence in medicine, willingness to give sympathy and understanding to patients who may be ill as a result of failure (in contrast to giving medical treatment), and tolerance of traditional medical practices. In all of these cases less tolerance is expressed for Moroccan than for Rumanian patients.

Several possible reasons for such differential orientations have been suggested. One concerns the greater conformity of Rumanian patients to the norms of expected Western patient behavior. There is evidence that physicians believe Moroccan patients to be more frequent malingerers; in fact, Moroccans are in greater need of formal certificates attesting to legitimate illness. We have also suggested that certain weak but widespread norms of prejudice exist in the society and some of these may have been internalized by physicians who express them in a differential orientation toward the two ethnic groups of patients. It is also important to recall that the doctors themselves are overwhelmingly European and therefore culturally closer to the Rumanians. Finally we have noted that pressures from the bureaucratically organized medical organization could result in a generalized frustration which, in a general context of prejudice, could displace physicians' aggression onto Moroccan patients.

Physicians may feel less bound by universalistic norms of the profession when reporting about the above areas which appear to be less medically relevant. However, it is certainly of interest that doctors were willing to express such differential orientations openly in a written questionnaire. These candid statements suggest that there could be a carry-over of differential orientations to the behavioral sphere.

The overall effect of these different patterns of orientation is not entirely clear. One possibility is that physicians could be motivated to be especially conscientious in their medical treatment of Moroccan patients—in a conscious or unconscious effort to compensate for differential orientations in nonmedical areas. Such an approach represents a form of "positive prejudice." On the other hand, it would probably be quite difficult to compartmentalize behavior and attitudes in a situation as complex as the doctor-patient relationship, so that one wonders whether physicians can really succeed in expressing greater tolerance and understanding of one group in areas unrelated directly to diagnosis and treatment while at the same time dispensing equal treatment in the medical care of the two groups.

Furthermore there would seem to be some doubt as to the greater medical relevance of some elements of the physician's behavior in the clinic situation, as compared to others. From the broadest point of view, one might argue that everything the physician does in his relationship with the patient has medical relevance —in terms of the latter's feelings, rapport, and potential curability. Even if one takes a less extreme position, it is certainly problematical to define just which elements in the physician's behavior have direct medical relevance and which do not.

These findings become even more meaningful when we consider them against the background of expressed need by the ethnic groups. Moroccan and Rumanian clients are characterized by different levels of the five needs observed. Differential response patterns by physicians must be considered in terms of these general patterns.

While Moroccans and Rumanians show a more or less equal need for catharsis, the two groups differ with respect to the four other needs: Moroccans report a feeling of failure somewhat more frequently than Rumanians, they more often express a need for status, traditional medical beliefs are more prevalent among them, and they are more concerned to move out of the confines of their own ethnic group into Israeli society.

A certain equilibrium may be said to exist with respect to the latent function of catharsis-giving: the two ethnic groups report equal need while physicians state that they respond equally to the two groups of patients. While we are unable to judge whether the absolute level of catharsis-giving is adequate to completely satisfy the groups of patients, at least there is no evident disequilibrium—with one patient group obtaining more of the latent function than the other.

With respect to the other four latent functions we find an invidious disequilibrium, with physicians responding more to the group showing a comparatively lower level of need. Thus we find physicians responding with greater sympathy and understanding to Rumanians than to Moroccans in the areas of status-giving, over-confidence in medicine, illness as a result of failure, and tolerance of traditional medical practices. In all of these areas Moroccans show a higher level of need than Rumanians. This disequilibrium not only violates the universalistic norm of medical practice, but works to the disadvantage of the group with the higher need.

GUIDELINES FOR RESEARCH

From a general sociological point of view it is worth noting that there are few if any empirical studies of the latent functions of social institutions reported in the literature (Merton, 1949; Brede-meier, 1955). While the theoretical formulations concerning this phenomenon are persuasive, it remains to establish the more precise empirical nature and structuring of the latent functions of different social institutions. This study represents a modest effort in that direction.

Future research could expand the approach taken here in two directions: intensive—by additional study of the same or other latent functions of the medical institution, and extensive—by a study of the latent functions of other social institutions.

The five latent functions of the medical institution studied here are not the only ones that could be investigated. We selected them because of their inherent interest and because of their special relevance in an immigrant society. Other latent functions of the medical institution could be studied in the Israeli context. A more complete picture would be obtained through a study in other societies of medical institutions characterized by similar or different latent functions. Replication and expansion of the study of latent functions of medical institutions would contribute to the growing field of medical sociology.

On a more general sociological level, the present research could be expanded to a study of latent functions of other social institutions. Such an expansion shifts the focus from the specific area of medical sociology to the more general sociological implications of latent functions. Some of the same latent functions studied here could be considered in the context of other social institutions—either in Israel or elsewhere. We have been interested in clients' choice of the medical institution to satisfy needs; study of other social institutions in the Israeli context could shed light on the circumstances under which alternative social institutions are utilized to satisfy the same needs.

Another direction in which the present research could be expanded is by the inclusion of additional and culturally different client groups. The Kurds, who were the most traditional of the groups included in our study, provided some especially interesting findings concerning perception and utilization patterns. In order to substantiate these more fully, it would seem worth studying other traditional groups—fairly quickly, before the acculturation process moves them too far away from their indigenous cultural patterns.

At the other end of the continuum, it would be useful to study additional westernized groups in order to determine which, if any, latent functions are relevant to them. The findings of the present study show the medical institution to be performing its latent functions particularly for the more traditional segments of the population. This finding could be a result of the specific latent functions on which we focused; it would therefore seem fruitful to study the kinds of latent functions which are salient to the more Westernized segments of the population.

Our research strategy has focused on clients' reports of need satisfaction by the institution as the major source of evidence for the existence and functioning of the latent functions. One of the weaker links in our chain of analysis has been the measurement of this need satisfaction. It would seem feasible that in some cases unclear results might be a result of poor measurement techniques. We have already noted it would be a good deal easier for Merton (1949) to measure the extent to which food baskets are distributed to low income families by political parties than it is for us to estimate the extent to which clients satisfy a need for status or integration through a medical institution. Believing as we do that information on such need satisfaction must be obtained from the client himself, it becomes necessary to devise some strategy that makes possible an ordering of clients on their feeling of need satisfaction by the institution. This is particularly difficult with complex, social-psychological needs of the sort we have considered here. Yet these are precisely the types of needs that are often satisfied through the latent functions of many social institutions. The problem therefore has some generality and is not limited to the research reported here. One direction for future research could be to improve and sharpen both the strategy and method used to measure clients' feelings concerning need satisfaction by the institution. Our impression is that more than one variable might be needed to probe various dimensions of need satisfaction.

Another improvement would be to base the analysis of clinic utilization rates on reliable records rather than on clients' reports. We are aware of the limitations of the approach used here and have attempted to spell them out in Chapter Four. While we do not believe that use of reported frequency of utilization has resulted in major distortions in our findings, it would undoubtedly be desirable to base the analysis on reliably kept records of clients' clinic visits. Part of a future research undertaking in this field might include improved record keeping to make possible an analysis based on such records. Needless to say, such record keeping would have to cover a sufficient number of clients to make possible appropriate selection of populations for study.[1]

Along the same lines, it would be worth using clinical and

---

[1] This has been attempted in Britain. See Bierman, et al., 1968,

objective evaluations of respondents' health instead of self-evalua-
tions by the subjects of study. Since clinic utilization is a major
dependent variable in the analysis, a reasonably objective evaluation of health would seem to be essential. The present research had
no alternative but to use respondents' own estimate: while this is
probably correlated with a clinical evaluation, we are unable to
judge the precise size of the correlation or the nature of its variation
in subgroups of the population.

Furthermore this problem is intensified by our use of the
tendency variable. It will be recalled that the tendency to define
oneself as ill is a subjective variable which plays a major role in the
paradigm testing the hypotheses of the study. There is an obvious
relationship between this tendency variable and subjects' self-
evaluations of their own health status. This is an additional reason
to obtain clinical and objective evaluations of health in a future
research undertaking.

The two sets of data on which the study is based—from
Kupat Holim members and physicians—were gathered separately
and not individually matched. Physicians' response was estimated
from statements concerning their attitudes and orientation to the
ethnic groups rather than in terms of specific cases of interaction.
The resources available to the present research did not permit the
complex field operation required for a completely matched sample
of patients and their specific physicians. In order to carry out a
systematic matching of the two populations it is necessary as a first
stage to locate a sufficient number of doctors who treat fifty or more
patients a year—or whatever number is determined to be sufficient
—of each ethnic group. Specific interactions must then be rated,
either by observation or reporting, first in terms of level of client
need and then by the nature of physician's response. The unit of
analysis becomes the interaction unit which is jointly categorized in
terms of client's need and physician's response. A comparison of the
distribution of such interaction units among physicians treating
different ethnic groups serves as the basis of the analysis. While this
procedure is complex as well as costly, it would seem to be worth
trying.

Measurement of physicians' response in the present study is
based on doctors' reports of their behavior within the framework

of a questionnaire. We have already noted that such an approach can hardly prevent distortions in reporting, particularly in the direction of conformity to professional norms. Another approach would measure response by direct observation of the doctor-patient relationship in a clinic situation. Rather than basing the analysis on subjects' statements *about* their behavior, such an approach focuses directly on the behavior itself. Undoubtedly this procedure involves difficulties of its own, possibly no less complex than those of questionnaire-based information: prolonged observation in order to obtain a sufficient number of cases, definition of categories of observation as well as systematic methods of counting, bias or change in both physician and patient behavior as a result of the presence of observers. Despite these formidable difficulties, it would seem worth investing the time and effort needed to gather data directly from the behavioral context.

Bibliography

ANDERSON, O. W., and SHEATSLEY, P. B. *Comprehensive Medical Insurance.* Research Series 9. New York: Health Information Foundation, 1959.

ANDERSON, O. W. "The Utilization of Health Services," in Freeman, H. E. Levine, S., and Reeder, L. G. (Eds.), *Handbook of Medical Sociology.* Englewood Cliffs, N.J.: Prentice-Hall, 1963.

ANDERSON, O. W., COLLETTE, P., and FELDMAN, J. J. *Change in Family Medical Care Expenditures and Voluntary Health Insurance.* Cambridge, Mass.: Harvard University Press, 1963.

BACKETT, E. M., HEADY, J. A., and EVANS, C. G. "Studies of a General Practice (11)—The Doctor's Job in an Urban Area," *British Medical Journal,* 1954, *1,* 109–115.

BALINT, M. "The Drug, 'Doctor,'" in Scott, W. R. and Volkart, E. H. (Eds.), *Medical Care.* New York: Wiley, 1966.

BELLOC, N. B. "Validation of Morbidity Surveys by Comparison with Hospital Records," *Journal of American Statistical Association,* 1954 (December), *49,* 832–846.

BEN-DAVID, J. "The Professional Role of the Physician in Bureaucratized Medicine," *Human Relations,* 1958, *11,* 255–274.

BENDIX, R., and LIPSET, S. M. *Class, Status, and Power: A Reader in Social Stratification.* (Rev. ed.) New York: Free Press, 1966.

BERLE, B. B. *Eighty Puerto Rican Families in New York City.* New York: Columbia University Press, 1958.

BIERMAN, P., et al. "Health Services Research in Great Britain," *Milbank Memorial Fund Quarterly,* 1968 (January, Part 1), *46*(1), 33.

BLOOM, S. *The Doctor and His Patient.* New York: Free Press, 1965.

BREDEMEIER, H. C. "The Methodology of Functionalism," *American Sociological Review,* 1955 (April), *20*(2), 173–180.

BROTHERSTON, J. H. F., and CHAVE, S. P. W. "General Practice in a New Housing Estate," *British Journal of Preventive and Social Medicine,* 1956 (October), *10*(4), 200–207.

BROWNE, K., and FREELING, P. "A Basic Misunderstanding," *Lancet,* 1965 (April), 803–805.

California, Department of Public Health. *Health and Medical Care Status of Californians.* The California Health Survey, 1958. State of California, Department of Public Health, 1966 (January).

CARTWRIGHT, A. *Patients and Their Doctors: A Study of General Practice.* London: Routledge and Kegan Paul, 1967.

COADY, A. "The Registrar in Out-Patients," *Lancet,* 1955, *269*(2), 430–432.

COHEN, J., MASSRY, S., DAVIES, A. M., MOOALEM, F., ARNON, A., WEISKOPF, P., VARON, M., and PARDESS, J. *Morbidity in Immigrant Villages: Doctor-Patient and Nurse-Patient Contacts in Eight Villages over Three Years.* Jerusalem: Ministry of Health and Department of Medical Ecology, Hebrew University-Hadassah Medical School, 1967 (mimeographed).

COLLINS, S. D. "Sickness Surveys," in Emerson, H. (Ed.) *Administrative Medicine.* New York: Nelson, 1951.

Columbia University, School of Public Health and Administrative Medicine. *Family Medical Care Under Three Types of Medical Insurance.* New York: Standard Press and Graphics, 1962.

CROOG, S. H. "Ethnic Origins, Educational Level and Responses to a Health Questionnaire," *Human Organization,* 1961 (Summer), *20*, 65–69.

DARSKY, B. J., SINAI, N., and AXELROD, S. J. *Comprehensive Medical Services Under Voluntary Health Insurance: A Study of Windsor Medical Services.* Cambridge, Mass.: Harvard University Press, 1958.

DOWNES, J., and MERTZ, J. "Effects of Frequency of Family Visiting upon the Reporting of Minor Illnesses," *Milbank Memorial Fund Quarterly*, 1953, *21*, 371–390.

ELINSON, J., and TRUSSELL, R. E. "Some Factors Relating Degree of Correspondence for Diagnostic Information as Obtained by Household Interviews and Clinical Examination," *American Journal of Public Health*, 1957, *47*, 311–321.

FEITELSON, D. *Educational Patterns of Kurdish Jews*. (Ph.D. dissertation) Jerusalem: Hebrew University, 1954.

FELDMAN, J. J. "Barriers to the Use of Health Survey Data in Demographic Analysis," *Milbank Memorial Fund Quarterly*, 1958 (July), *36*(3).

FELDMAN, J. J. "The Household Interview Survey as a Technique for the Collection of Morbidity Data," *Journal of Chronic Diseases*, 1960 (May), *11*(5), 535–557.

FELDMAN, J. J. *The Dissemination of Health Information*. Chicago: Aldine, 1966.

FELDSTEIN, P. J. "Research on the Demand for Health Services," *Milbank Memorial Fund Quarterly*, 1966 (July, Part 2), *44*, 3.

FIELD, M. *Doctor and Patient in Soviet Russia*. Cambridge, Mass.: Harvard University Press, 1957.

FIELD, M. *Soviet Socialized Medicine*. New York: Free Press, 1967.

FLETCHER, C. M. "Some Problems of Diagnostic Standardization Using Clinical Methods, with Special Reference to Chronic Bronchitis," in Pemberton, J. (Ed.), *Epidemiology Reports on Research and Teaching, 1962*. London: Oxford University Press, 1963.

FORSYTH, G. *Doctors and State Medicine, A Study of the British Health Services*. London: Pitman, 1964.

FREIDSON, E. "Client Control and Medical Practice," *American Journal of Sociology*, 1960, *65*, 374–382.

FREIDSON, E. *Patients' View of Medical Practice*. New York: Russell Sage Foundation, 1961.

FRY, J. "A Year of General Practice: A Study in Morbidity," *British Medical Journal*, 1952, 2, 249–252.

GAMSON, W. A., and SCHUMAN, H. "Some Undercurrents in the Prestige of Physicians," *American Journal of Sociology*, 1963 (January), *68*, 463–470.

GANS, H. J. *The Urban Villagers*. New York: Free Press, 1962.

GORDON, G. *Role Theory and Illness*. New Haven: College and University Press, 1966.

GRAY, P. G. "The Memory Factor in Social Surveys," *Journal of the American Statistical Association*, 1955, *50*, 344–363.

GRUSHKA, T. (Ed.). *Health Services in Israel.* Jerusalem: Ministry of Health, 1968.

HALEVI, M. S. "Health Services in Israel: Their Organization, Utilization and Financing," *Medical Care,* 1964 (October–December), 2, 4.

HANOCH, G. "Income Differentials in Israel," *Falk Project for Economic Research in Israel, Fifth Report, 1959 and 1960.* Jerusalem, 1961.

Health Information Foundation. "The Increased Use of Medical Care," *Progress in Health Services,* 1958 (October).

Health Insurance Plan of Greater New York. Committee for the Special Research Project. *Health and Medical Care in New York City.* Cambridge, Mass.: Harvard University Press, 1957.

Health Insurance Plan of Greater New York. *Statistical Report.* 1962.

HENDERSON, L. J. "Physician and Patient as a Social System," *New England Journal of Medicine,* 1935 (May), *212*(18), 819–823.

HES, J. P. "From Nature Healer to Modern Psychiatrist," *Israel Annals of Psychiatry,* 1964 (October), *2*(2), 192–208.

HILL, A. B. "The Doctor's Day and Pay," *Journal of the Royal Statistical Society,* 1951, *114*, 1.

HOGARTH, J. *The Payment of the General Practitioner.* Oxford: Pergamon Press, 1963.

INKELES, A., and ROSSI, P. H. "National Comparisons of Occupational Prestige," *American Journal of Sociology,* 1956 (January), *61*, 329–339.

International Labour Organization. *The Cost of Medical Care.* Geneva: 1959.

Israel Central Bureau of Statistics. *Statistical Abstract of Israel.* No. 12. Jerusalem: Government Printer, 1961.

Israel Central Bureau of Statistics. *Demographic Characteristics of the Population.* Part III, Publication No. 13, Jerusalem: Government Printer, 1963.

Israel Central Bureau of Statistics. *Statistical Abstract of Israel,* No. 18. Jerusalem: Government Printer, 1967.

Israel Ministry of Health. *Report of the Committee on the Doctor Shortage 1963–64* (Hebrew). Jerusalem: Government Printer, 1964.

KADUSHIN, C. "Social Class and the Experience of Ill Health," *Sociological Inquiry,* 1964 (Winter), *34*(1), 67–80.

KANEV, I. *Mutual Aid and Social Medicine in Israel.* Tel Aviv: Kupat Holim, 1965.

KASL, S. V., and COBB, S. "Health Behavior, Illness Behavior and Sick Role Behavior," *Archives of Environmental Health,* 1966 (February), *12.*

KATZ, E., and EISENSTADT, S. N. "Some Sociological Observations on the Response of Israeli Organizations to New Immigrants," *Administrative Science Quarterly,* 1960 (June), *5,* 113–133.

KEDWARD, H. B. "Social Class Habits of Consulting," *British Journal of Preventive and Social Medicine,* 1962, *16*(3), 147–152.

KING, S. H. *Perceptions of Illness and Medical Practice.* New York: Russell Sage Foundation, 1962.

KNUPFER, G. "Portrait of the Underdog," in Bendix, R., and Lipset, S. M. (Eds.), *Class, Status and Power.* New York: Free Press, 1953.

KOOS, E. *The Health of Regionville.* New York: Columbia University Press, 1954.

Kupat Holim, Department of Research and Statistics. *Statistical Report* (Hebrew), 1960 (September), *51*(1), 14.

Kupat Holim, Department of Research and Statistics. *Frequency of Utilization, Research in Kubeiba Clinic* (Hebrew). Tel Aviv: 1961 (mimeographed).

Kupat Holim. *Figures on Kupat Holim Physicians, April 1961* (Hebrew). Tel Aviv: 1962.

Kupat Holim, Department of Research and Statistics. *Statistical Bulletin* (Hebrew). 1964a (December), *2*(3), 38.

Kupat Holim, National Supervising Committee, Efficiency and Savings Sub-Committee. *Working Organization of General Physicians in Tel-Aviv, Jaffa and Haifa Districts* (Hebrew). Tel Aviv: General Federation of Labor, Survey No. 10, 1964b (July).

Kupat Holim, Department of Research and Statistics. *Statistical Bulletin.* (Hebrew) 1965 (December), *5,* 6, p. 32.

Kupat Holim, Department of Research and Statistics. "The Clinic as a Center for Medical-Social Care," *Studies and Surveys* (Hebrew). Tel Aviv: 1966 (November), *39.*

Kupat Holim, Department of Research and Statistics. "In-Patient Morbidity Inquiry in Kupat Holim Hospitals for the Years 1963–64," *Studies and Surveys* (Hebrew). Tel Aviv: 1967 (July), *41.*

LEES, D. S., and COOPER, M. H. "The Work of the General Practitioner," *Journal of the College of General Practitioners,* 1963, *6*(408), 411.

LEVINE, G. N. "Anxiety about Illness," *Journal of Health and Human Behavior,* 1962 (Spring), *3*(1), 30–34.

LEVY, M. J., JR. *The Structure of Society.* Princeton, N.J.: Princeton University Press, 1952.

LIEBERSON, S. "Ethnic Groups and the Practice of Medicine," *American Sociological Review,* 1958 (October), *23,* 542–549.

LISSAK, M. "Trends in the Integration of Immigrants in the Class and Political System of Israel," in *Mizug Galuyot* (Hebrew). Jerusalem: Magnes Press, 1969.

LOGAN, R. F. L., and EIMERL, T. S. "Case Loads in Hospital and General Practice in Several Countries," *Milbank Memorial Fund Quarterly,* 1965 (April, Part 2), *43,* 309.

LOGAN, W. P. D. *Studies on Medical and Population Subjects, No. 7 and 14.* London: Her Majesty's Stationer's Office, 1957.

LOGAN, W. P. D., and BROOKE, E. M. "The Survey of Sickness, 1943 to 1952," *Studies on Medical and Population Subjects, No. 12.* London: Her Majesty's Stationer's Office, 1957.

MACGREGOR, F. C. *Social Science in Nursing.* New York: Wiley, 1965.

MARTIN, J. P. *Social Aspects of Prescribing.* London: William Heinemann, 1957.

MATRAS, J. *Social Change in Israel.* Chicago: Aldine Press, 1965.

MECHANIC, D. "The Concept of Illness Behavior," *Journal of Chronic Diseases,* 1962, *15,* 189–194.

MECHANIC, D. "Religion, Religiosity, and Illness Behavior: The Special Case of the Jews," *Human Organization,* 1963 (Fall), *22*(3), 202–203.

MECHANIC, D. *Medical Sociology.* New York: Free Press, 1968.

MECHANIC, D., and VOLKART, E. A. "Illness Behavior and Medical Diagnosis," *Journal of Health and Human Behavior,* 1960, *1*(2), 86–94.

MECHANIC, D., and VOLKART, E. A. "Stress, Illness, and the Sick Role," *American Sociological Review,* 1961 (February), 51–58.

MERTON, R. K. *Social Theory and Social Structure.* New York: Free Press, 1949.

MORAG, P. *Doctor and Patient: Bureaucrat and Client* (M.A. thesis, Hebrew). Department of Sociology, Hebrew University of Jerusalem, 1966.

MORRIS, J. N. *Uses of Epidemiology,* Second Edition. Edinburgh: Livingstone, 1964.

MOSES, R., and HOEK, A. "Uses and Abuses of Medical Certificates," *Israel Medical Journal,* 1961, *20*(3–4), 95–102.

MURRAY, D. S. "The National Health Service in Britain," in *Medical Care and Family Security.* Englewood Cliffs, N.J.: Prentice-Hall, 1963.

NALL, F. C., II, and SPIELBERG, J. "Social and Cultural Factors in the Responses of Mexican-Americans to Medical Treatment," *Journal of Health and Social Behavior,* 1967 (December), *8*(4), 299–308.

National Opinion Research Center. "Jobs and Occupations: A Popular Evaluation," in Bendix, R., and Lipset, S. M. (Eds.), *Class, Status and Power.* New York: Free Press, 1953.

NEIMAN, I. S. "The General Practitioner in Prepaid Group Practice Plans," *American Journal of Public Health,* 1963 (October), *53,* 1635–1643.

PARSONS, T. *The Social System.* New York: Free Press, 1951.

PARSONS, T. "Definitions of Health and Illness in the Light of American Values and Social Structure," in Jaco, E. (Ed.), *Patients, Physicians and Illness.* New York: Free Press, 1958.

PHILLIPS, D. "Self-Reliance and the Inclination to Adopt the Sick Role," *Social Forces,* 1965, *43,* 555–563.

POPON, C. "Standards of Hospitalization and Health Needs of the Population of the U.S.S.R.," paper presented at the Symposium on Hospital and Domiciliary Medical Care, WHO, Amsterdam, November 1962.

PUROLA, T., KALIMO, E., SIEVERS, K., and NYMAN, K. *The Utilization of the Medical Services and Its Relationship to Morbidity, Health Resources, and Social Factors.* Helsinki: Research Institute for Social Security, 1968.

ROEMER, M. I. *Medical Care in Latin America.* Washington, D.C.: Organization of American States, General Secretariat, Pan American Union, 1963.

ROGLER, L. H., and HOLLINGSHEAD, A. B. *Trapped.* New York: Wiley, 1965.

ROSENBLATT, D., and SUCHMAN, E. A. "Blue-Collar Attitudes and Information toward Health and Illness," in Shostak, A. B., and Gomberg, W. (Eds.), *Blue-Collar World.* Englewood Cliffs, N.J.: Prentice-Hall, 1964.

ROSENSTOCK, I. M. "Why People Use Health Services," *Milbank Memorial Fund Quarterly,* 1966 (July, Part 2), *44*(3).

SA'ADIA, H. *Utilization of the General Practitioner in an Immigrant Town* (Hebrew, unpublished survey). Beersheba: Kupat Holim, 1965.

SANDERS, B. S. "Have Morbidity Surveys Been Oversold?" *American Journal of Public Health,* 1962, *52*(10), 1648–1659.

SANDERS, I. T. "Public Health in the Community," in Freeman, H. E., Levine, S., and Reeder, L. G. (Eds.), *Handbook of Medical Sociology.* Englewood Cliffs, N.J.: Prentice-Hall, 1963.

SHIPMAN, G. A., LAMPMAN, R. J., and MIYAMOTO, S. F. *Medical Service Corporations in the State of Washington: A Study of the Administration of Physician-Sponsored Prepaid Medical Care.* Cambridge, Mass.: Harvard University Press, 1962.

SHOSTAK, A., and GOMBERG, W. (Eds.) *Blue Collar World.* Englewood Cliffs, N.J.: Prentice-Hall, 1964.

SHUVAL, J. T. *Social Class and Ethnicity: A Study in Social Structure and Interpersonal Relations* (Ph.D. dissertation). Radcliffe College, 1955.

SHUVAL, J. T. "Patterns of Inter-Group Tension and Affinity," *International Social Science Bulletin,* 1956, *8*(1), 75–123.

SHUVAL, J. T. "Emerging Patterns of Ethnic Strain in Israel," *Social Forces,* 1962a, *40,* 323–330; and in Barron, M. L. (Ed.), *Minorities in a Changing World.* New York: Knopf, 1967.

SHUVAL, J. T. "Ethnic Stereotyping in Israeli Medical Bureaucracies," *Sociology and Social Research,* 1962b, *46*(4).

SHUVAL, J. T. *Immigrants on the Threshold.* New York: Atherton Press, 1963.

SHUVAL, J. T. "Self-Rejection among North African Immigrants to Israel," *The Israel Annals of Psychiatry and Related Disciplines,* 1966 (Spring), *4*(1), 101–110.

SHUVAL, J. T., ANTONOVSKY, A., and DAVIES, A. M. "The Doctor-Patient Relationship in an Ethnically Heterogeneous Society," *Social Science and Medicine,* 1967, *1,* 141–154.

SILVER, G. A. *Family Medical Care.* Cambridge, Mass.: Harvard University Press, 1963a.

SILVER, G. A. *Report on World Health Organization Sponsored Trip to Norway, Yugoslavia, Czechoslovakia, and Poland.* New York: Montefiore Hospital, 1963b.

SILVER, G. A., CHERKASKY, M., and AXELROD, J. "An Experience with Group Practice: The Montefiore Medical Group, 1948–1956," *New England Journal of Medicine,* 1957 (April), *256,* 785–791.

SIMMONS, O. G. "The Clinical Team in a Chilean Health Center," in Paul, B. D. (Ed.), *Health, Culture and Community.* New York: Russell Sage Foundation, 1955.

SIMMONS, O. G. "Implications of Social Class for Public Health," in Jaco, E. G. (Ed.), *Patients, Physicians and Illness*. New York: Free Press, 1958a.

SIMMONS, O. G. *Social Status and Public Health*. Social Science Research Council Pamphlet No. 13. New York: Social Science Research Council, 1958b.

SIMMONS, W. R., and BRYANT, E. E. "An Evaluation of Hospitalization Data from the Health Interview Survey," *American Journal of Public Health*, 1962 (October), *52*, 1638–1647.

SIMON, A. J. "Social Structure and Patient Improvement," in Scott, W. R., and Volkart, E. H. (Eds.), *Medical Care*. New York: Wiley, 1966.

SOLON, J. A., SHEPS, C. G., LEE, S. S., and BARBANO, J. P. "Patterns of Medical Care: Validity of Interview Information on Use of Hospital Clinics," *Journal of Health and Human Behavior*, 1962 (Spring), *3*, 21–29.

STEIN, L. "Morbidity in a London General Practice: Social and Demographic Data," *British Journal of Preventive and Social Medicine*, 1960, *14*(1), 9–15.

STEVENSON, J. S. K. "General Practice in Scotland—Why the Difference? A Comparative Study of Statistics from Practices in the United Kingdom," *British Medical Journal*, 1964 (May), *1*, 1370–1373.

STOEKLE, J. D., and DAVIDSON, G. E. "Communicating Aggrieved Feelings in the Patient's Initial Visit to a Medical Clinic," *Journal of Health and Human Behavior*, 1963 (Fall), *4*(3), 199–206.

STOEKLE, J. D., ZOLA, I. K., and DAVIDSON, G. E. "On Going to See the Doctor: The Contributions of the Patient to the Decision to Seek Medical Aid, a Selected Review," *Journal of Chronic Diseases*, 1963, *16*, 975–989.

STOEKLE, J. D., ZOLA, I. K., and DAVIDSON, G. E. "The Quantity and Significance of Psychological Distress in Medical Patients," *Journal of Chronic Diseases*, 1964, *17*, 965–966.

SUCHMAN, E. A., PHILLIPS, B. S., and STREIB, G. F. "An Analysis of the Validity of Health Questionnaires," *Social Forces*, 1958 (March), *36*, 223–232.

SUCHMAN, E. A. "Sociomedical Variations among Ethnic Groups," *American Journal of Sociology*, 1964 (November), *70*(3), 319–331.

SUCHMAN, E. A. "Social Patterns of Illness and Medical Care," *Journal of Health and Human Behavior*, 1965a (Spring), *6*, 2–16.

SUCHMAN, E. A. "Stages of Illness and Medical Care," *Journal of Health and Human Behavior,* 1965b (Fall), 114–128.

SUCHMAN, E. A. "Health Orientation and Medical Care," *American Journal of Public Health,* 1966 (January), 97–105.

SZASZ, T. S., and HOLLENDER, M. H. "A Contribution to the Philosophy of Medicine," *Archives of Internal Medicine,* 1956 (May). 97, 585–592.

TAYLOR, S. *Good General Practice.* London: Nuffield Hospitals Trust, Oxford University Press, 1954.

TODD, J. W. "The Superior Clinical Acumen of the Old Physicians," *Lancet,* 1953, *264*(1), 482–484.

TRUSSELL, R. E., and ELINSON, J. *Chronic Illness in a Rural Area, The Hunterdon Study, 3,* Cambridge, Mass.: Harvard University Press, 1959.

United Kingdom Central Office of Information. *Health Services in Britain.* Reference Pamphlet No. 20. London: Her Majesty's Stationer's Office, 1964.

United Nations, Statistical Office. *United Nations Demographic Yearbook, 1963.* Fifteenth Issue. New York: 1964.

United Nations, Statistical Office. *United Nations Demographic Yearbook, 1964.* Sixteenth Issue. New York: 1965.

U.S. National Health Survey, National Center for Health Statistics. *Reporting of Hospitalization in the Health Interview Survey.* Washington, D.C.: 1961, Series D-4.

U.S. National Health Survey, National Center for Health Statistics. *Medical Care, Health Status, and Family Income, U.S.* Washingon, D.C.: 1964, Series 10, No. 9.

U.S. National Health Survey, National Center for Health Statistics. *Volume of Physician Visits by Place of Visit and Type of Service, U.S., July 1963–June 1964.* Washington, D.C.: 1964, Series 10, No. 18.

U.S. National Health Survey, National Center for Health Statistics. *Health Interview Responses Compared wih Medical Records, Vital and Health Statistics, Data Evaluation and Methods Research.* Washington, D.C.: 1965, Series 2, No. 7.

VACEK, M. "Information on Morbidity from Medical Practice," in *Trends in the Study of Morbidity and Mortality.* Geneva: World Health Organization, 1965.

VAN DEEN, K. J. "Primary Medical Care. 2, Analysis of the Work Load," *Milbank Memorial Fund Quarterly,* 1965 (April, Part 2), *43,* 280.

VELDHOYZEN VAN ZANTEN, R. C. "Work of General Practitioners in Holland," *World Health Organization Expert Committee on General Practice*. Geneva: 1963.

VUKMANOVIC, C. "The System and Statistics in Yugoslavia Compared with Other Countries," *Milbank Memorial Fund Quarterly*, 1965 (April, Part 2), *43*, 296.

WAMOSCHER, Z. "Consultations in General Practice," *Dapim Refu'iim* (Hebrew), 1964 (April), *23*, 105–116.

WEBER, A. "Some Characteristics of Mortality and Morbidity in Europe," in Public Health Papers, No. 27, *Trends in the Study of Morbidity and Mortality*. Geneva: World Health Organization, 1965.

WEINBERG, A. A. *Migration and Belonging*. The Hague: Martinus Nijhoff, 1961.

WEINERMAN, E. R. "Patients' Perceptions of Group Medical Care," *American Journal of Public Health, 54*(6), 883.

WHITE, K. L., and JELKOVIC, D., et al., "International Comparisons of Medical Care Utilization," *New England Journal of Medicine*, 1967, *277*, 516–522.

WITTS, L. J. (Ed.) *Medical Surveys and Clinical Trials*, Second Edition. London: Oxford University Press, 1964.

World Health Organization. *Annual and Epidemiological Year Book, 1961*. Geneva: 1964.

World Health Organization, Regional Office for Europe. *Health Services in Europe*. Copenhagen: 1965a.

World Health Organization. *World Health Statistics Annual, 1962*. Volume 1, "Vital Statistics and Causes of Death." Geneva, 1965b.

WULMAN, L. *Oif Der Vakh fun Yidishn Folksgesunt* (Yiddish) (Guarding the Health of the Jewish People: Fifteen Years of "TOZ"). Warsaw: T-wo Ochrony Ludnosci Zydowskiej, 1937.

ZBOROWSKI, M. "Cultural Components in Response to Pain," *Journal of Social Issues*, 1952, *8*, 16–30.

ZBOROWSKI, M., and HERZOG, E. *Life is With People*. New York: International Universities Press, 1952.

ZBOROWSKI, M. *People in Pain*. San Francisco: Jossey-Bass, 1969.

ZOLA, I. K. "Illness Behavior of the Working Class: Implications and Recommendations," in Shostak, A., and Gomberg, W. (Eds.), *Blue Collar World*. Englewood Cliffs, N.J.: Prentice-Hall, 1964.

ZOLA, I. K. "Culture and Symptoms: An Analysis of Patients' Presenting Complaints," *American Sociological Review*, 1966, *31*, 615–630.

Selected Ethnographic Bibliography

KURDISH IMMIGRANTS

BAHARAV, G. "The Jews of Kurdistan," *Israel Youth Horizon,* 1966, 7(5).

BENAYAHU, M. Y. "Shmuel Barzani: Head of the Kurdish Jewish Community," *Sefinot* (Hebrew), *9,* 21–125.

BEN-YAACOV, A. *Kurdish Jewish Communities* (Hebrew). Jerusalem: Ben-Zvi Institute, Kiryet Sefer, 1961.

BRAVER, A. *The Jews of Kurdistan* (Hebrew). Jerusalem: Palestine Institute for Folklore and Ethnography, 1948.

FISCHEL, W. J. "The Jews of Kurdistan," *Commentary,* December 1949.

HAAS, W. S. *Iran.* London: Oxford University Press, 1946.

NIKITINE, B. *Les Kurdes, Etude Sociologique et Historique*. Paris: Klincksieck, 1956.

QUBAIN, F. I. *The Reconstruction of Iraq: 1950–1957*. New York: Praeger, 1958.

ROBINSON, N. *Persia and Afghanistan and Their Jewish Communities*. New York: Institute of Jewish Affairs, World Jewish Congress, 1953.

MOROCCAN IMMIGRANTS

BAUM, P., and POSTER, H. "The Jewish Crisis in Morocco," *Congress Bi-Weekly*, 1961 (February), *28*.

Central Bureau of Statistics. *Demographic Characteristics of the Population*. Jerusalem: 1963.

COHN, H. *Moeurs des Juifs et des Arabes de Tetuan (Maroc)*; *Avec une Lettre de S. Mun*, Deuxième Edition. Paris: Lipschutz, 1927.

CHOURAQUI, A. *Le Condition Juridique de l'Israelite Marocain*. Paris: Presse de Livre Francais, 1950.

CHOURAQUI, A. *Les Juifs d'Afrique du Nord, Marche vers l'Occident*. Paris: Presses Universitaires de France, 1952.

CHOURAQUI, A. "North African Jewry Today," *Jewish Journal of Sociology*, April 1959.

DONAT, D. *L'Evolution de la Femme Israelite à Fes*. Paris: La Pensée Universitaire, 1962.

FLAMAND, P. "Diaspora en Terre d'Islam—Les Communautés Israelites du Sud Marocain," Thèse de Doctorat, editée par les Imprimeries Réunies. Casablanca: 1959.

ISRAEL, G. "L'Alliance Israelite Universelle," *Cahiers de l'Alliance Israelite Universelle*, Paris, Fevrier 1960.

JACOBS, M. *A Study of Cultural Stability and Change: The Moroccan Jewess*. Washington, D.C.: Catholic University of America Press, 1956.

LANDSHUT, S. *Jewish Communities in the Moslem Countries of the Middle East*. Survey prepared for the American-Jewish Committee and the Anglo-Jewish Association. London: The Jewish Chronicle, 1950.

LEHRMAN, H. "North Africa's Dilemma for American Jewry," *Commentary*, March 1951.

LEHRMAN, H. "Morocco's Jews Between Islam and France," *Commentary*, November 1956.

LESTCHINSKY, J. "The Economic Development of Jews in the Moslem

Countries," in Dinur, B., Tartakover, A., and Lestchinsky, J. *The Jewish Community: Selections on the Sociology of the Jewish People* (Hebrew). Jerusalem: Mosad Bialik, 1954.

MALKA, E. *Essai Ethnographie Traditionelle des Mellahs* (Rabat, typ. "Omnia," 1946).

SLOUSCHZ, N. *The Jews of North Africa*. Philadelphia: The Jewish Publication Society of America (5704), 1944.

POLISH IMMIGRANTS

American Jewish Yearbook. The Jewish Publication Society of America, Vol. 47, 48, 51, 66.

BERGMAN, M. "Return to Poland," *Commentary*, May 1959.

BRONSZTEJN, S. "The Jewish Population of Poland," *Jewish Journal of Sociology*, 1964 (July), 6(1).

Central Bureau of Statistics. *Demographic Characteristics of the Population*. Jerusalem: 1963.

HALEVI, H. S. "The Demography of Jewish Communities in Eastern Europe," *Jewish Journal of Sociology*, 1960 (June), 2(1).

The Jewish Population in Poland (Hebrew). Warsaw: Jewish Cultural Association of Poland, 1955.

Jews in Poland, Volume 1 (Hebrew). Jerusalem: Youth Department, World Zionist Organization, 1948.

LESTCHINSKY, J. *The Jewish Exile* (Hebrew). Jerusalem: Department of Education and Culture of the World Zionist Organization, 1961.

LUCJAN, B. "Poland and the Jewish Remnant," *Commentary*, March 1957.

MEYER, P., WEINRYB, B. E., DUSCHINSKY, E., and SYLVIAN, N. *The Jews in the Soviet Satellites*. Syracuse, N.Y.: Syracuse University Press, 1963.

Poland in Figures (1944–1961). Central Statistical Office of the Polish Peoples' Republic. Warsaw: 1962.

POLIAKOFF, S. "Predecessors of the Modern OSE," *American OSE Review*, 1944, 3(1).

ROBINSON, N. *Poland After October*. New York: Institute of Jewish Affairs, World Jewish Congress, 1957.

RUPPIN, A. *The Jews in the Modern World*. London: Macmillan, 1934.

RUPPIN, A. "Sociology of Marriage among Jews," in Dinur, B., Tartakover, A., and Lestchinsky, J. *The Jewish Community: Selections on the Sociology of the Jewish People* (Hebrew). Jerusalem: Mosad Bialik, 1954.

SEGAL, S. *The New Poland and the Jews.* New York: Lee Furman, 1938.

The Jewish People, Past and Present, Vol. 2, Jewish Encyclopaedic Handbooks. New York: Central Yiddish Cultural Organization, 1948.

WULMAN, L. *Oif der Vakh fun Yidishin Folksgesunt* (Guarding The Health of the Jewish People. Fifteen Years of "TOZ"). Warsaw: T-wo Ochrony Ludnosci Zydowskiej w Polsce, 1937.

RUMANIAN IMMIGRANTS

American Jewish Yearbook. The Jewish Publication Society of America, Vol. 40, 51, 53, 55, 57, 62, 66.

American OSE Review. American Committee for Protection of the Health of the Jews, OSE Inc. New York, Vol. 3, 4, 5.

Central Bureau of Statistics. *Demographic Characteristics of the Population.* Jerusalem: 1963.

Contemporary Jewish Record, 1939 (September–October), 2(5).

HALEVI, H. S. "The Demography of Jewish Communities in Eastern Europe," *Jewish Journal of Sociology,* 1960 (June), 2(1).

HERBERT, E. *Roumania as I Found It.* New York: Gerard Press, 1924.

Jewish Observer Newsletter, No. 2, London, July 1958.

KAMLON-KOGAN, W. "Factors in the Immigration of Jews from Rumania, Galicia, and Russia," in Dinur, B., Tartakover, A., and Lestchinsky, J. *The Jewish Community: Selections on the Sociology of the Jewish People* (Hebrew). Jerusalem: Mosad Bialik, 1954.

MEYER, P., WEINRYB, B. D., DUSCHINSKY, E., and SYLVANIAN, N. *The Jews in the Soviet Satellites.* Syracuse, N.Y.: Syracuse University Press, 1953.

Rumanian Statistical Pocket Book 1964. Rumanian Peoples' Republic, Central Statistical Board.

RUPPIN, A. *The Jews in the Modern World.* London: Macmillan, 1934.

WEINRYB, B. D. "East European Jewry," in Finkelstein, L. (Ed.). *The Jews, Their History, Culture and Religion.* New York: Harper, 1960.

Index

A

Acculturation, 16, 127–143. *See also* Integration into Israeli society
African-origin immigrants, clinic attendance of, 73–74. *See also* Moroccans
Alliance Israelite Universelle, 45
Amidar, 123
ANDERSON, O. W., 64, 70
ARNON, A., 72, 74, 75
Asian-origin immigrants, clinic use by, 73–74. *See also* Kurds
AXELROD, S. J., 64

B

BACKETT, E. M., 112
BALINT, M., 92, 110
BARBANO, J. P., 70n
BELLOC, N. B., 70n
BEN-DAVID, J., 28
BENDIX, R., 144
BERLE, B. B., 10, 16, 111
BIERMAN, P., 64, 197n

BREDEMEIER, H. C., 13, 195
BROOKE, E. M., 70
BROTHERSTON, J. H. F., 64, 72
BROWNE, K., 5n
BRYANT, E. E., 70n

C

Catharsis needs, 13–15, 20, 91–109; and clinic use, 184–185, 189, 191–192; and ethnic origin, 97, 99, 106; and nurse, 94, 95–97, 99, 101, 106, 109; and physician, 94–95, 97–99, 102, 107, 108–109; physician's response to, 103–106, 107; testing of hypothesis of, 97, 99
Certification of illness, 11, 111–113. *See also* Petek
CHAVE, S. P. W., 64, 72
Client population studied, 4–5
Clinic personnel, ethnic group differences in perception of, 132–136

Clinic use: and acculturation, 75,
    79; by age and sex, 74–75; ca-
    tharsis needs vs. rate of, 99–
    103; comparison with in other
    countries, 63, 64, 78; data-
    gathering on, 197–199; and
    ethnic origin, 73–74; frequency
    of, 4, 5, 62–69, 74; high, 72–
    78, 78–79; latent functions of,
    23–24,   183–184,   190–192;
    overutilization, 23–24, 65, 68,
    183–184, 190–192; record-
    keeping on, 32, 69–72, 197; as
    reported by patients, 69–72,
    78; rural, 74; and size of
    family, 75, 78; suggested pay-
    ment scheme for, 68–69; un-
    derreporting of, 70–71, 78
COADY, A., 134
COBB, S., 20, 81
COHEN, J., 72, 74, 75
COLLETTE, P., 70
COLLINS, S. D., 70
Columbia University, School of
    Public Health and Adminis-
    trative Medicine, 64
COOPER, M. H., 72n
Coping with failure, 10, 15–16, 20,
    110–126; and clinic attend-
    ance, 115, 116, 118, 124–125,
    186–187, 189, 191–192; and
    petek-granting, 114–117, 124;
    physicians' response to, 118–
    123, 125–126; testing of hy-
    pothesis of, 116, 118; variables
    in, 113–114, 116, 123–124

D

DARSKY, B. J., 64
DAVIDSON, G. E., 15n, 110
DAVIES, A. M., 72, 74, 75
Dhimmi, 42–43
DOWNES, J., 70

E

Education and status needs, 145–147
EIMERL, T. S., 64
EISENSTADT, S. N., 4

ELINSON, J., 70, 70n
Equalitarianism in Israeli society, 26,
    145
Ethnic groups, comparison of clinic
    use by, 73–74
European immigrant groups: adop-
    tion of sick role by, 82; clinic
    use among, 73–74; low status
    needs of, 147; nurse and ca-
    tharsis needs of, 95, 97; per-
    ception of physician's status
    by, 148; and petek-granting,
    116, 125–126; view of clinic
    personnel by, 134. *See also*
    Poles; Rumanians
EVANS, C. G., 112

F

Failure, coping with, 110–126. *See
    also* Coping with failure
FEITELSON, D., 40
FELDMAN, J. J., 70, 70n, 144
FELDSTEIN, P. J., 61
FIELD, M., 26, 112
FLETCHER, C. M., 164
FREELING, P., 5n
FREIDSON, E., 27
French Protectorate in Morocco, 44–
    47
FRY, J., 112
Functions, latent, of medical insti-
    tutions, 190–192. *See also* Ca-
    tharsis needs; Coping with
    failure; Integration into Israeli
    society; Magic-science con-
    flicts; Status needs
Functions, social, of medical practice,
    181–199

G

Gaining status, 144–160. *See also*
    Status needs
GAMSON, W. A., 150
GANS, H. J., 145
General Federation of Labor (Hista-
    drut), 6, 9, 127, 128
GOMBERG, W., 86
GORDON, G., 10

GRAY, P. G., 70
GRUSHKA, T., 6, 9

H

HANOCH, G., 16, 17, 129–130
HEADY, J. A., 112
Health, national, comparison of with other countries, 63, 66–67
Health Insurance Plan of Greater New York, 64, 70n, 71
HENDERSON, L. J., 24
HERZOG, E., 9, 144
HES, J. P., 46n
HILL, A. B., 64
Histadrut (General Federation of Labor), 6, 9, 127, 128
HOEK, A., 11, 111, 112
HOGARTH, J., 64
HOLLENDER, M. H., 24

I

Illness: legitimation of, 111–113; rewards of, 81, 110–111, 112–113. *See also* Sick role
Immigrant populations: catharsis needs of, 13–15, 91–109; and coping with failure, 15–16, 110–126; high clinic use of, 190–191; integration of into Israeli society, 4–5, 16, 127–143; magic-science conflicts of, 17–19, 20, 161–178; needs and problems of, 13–19; sampling of ethnic groups of, 32–34; status needs of, 16–17, 144–160. *See also* Kurds; Moroccans; Poles; Rumanians
INKELES, A., 144
Integration into Israeli society, 16, 127–143; and clinic use, 127–128, 141–142, 187, 188–189, 190–191; comparison of need for, 130–132; of Europeans vs. non-Europeans, 129–130; physicians' response to efforts toward, 136–141, 142–143; role of Kupat Holim in, 127–128, 141–142; and shedding

ethnic identity, 128–130; testing of hypothesis of, 132–136
Israel Central Bureau of Statistics, 7, 33, 34, 62, 72, 72n
Israel Ministry of Health, 61–62

J

Jews, tendency of to adopt sick role, 82–83
Joint Distribution Committee program for Rumanian Jewry, 49–50

K

KADUSHIN, C., 86
KALIMO, E., 74
KANEV, I., 79, 127, 130
KASL, S. V., 20, 81
KATZ, E., 4
KEDWARD, H. B., 64
KING, S. H., 86, 161, 163
KNUPFER, G., 83, 85
KOOS, E., 81, 83n
Kupat Holim, 6–9, 35; and clinic attendance, 61–79; members selected for research study, 31–34; physicians selected for study, 34–35; role of in integration of immigrants, 127–128, 141–142
Kupat Holim, Department of Research and Statistics, 7, 62
Kupat Holim, National Supervising Committee, Efficiency and Savings Sub-committee, 7, 8
Kurds, 4, 32, 45–47, 56, 57; catharsis needs of and (a) clinic use, 108, 185, (b) nurse, 95–97, 106, 108, (c) physician, 97, 99, 108; date of immigration of, 56; education of, 41; ethnographic sketch of, 39–42; feeling of failure of, 114, 116; high clinic use among, 73, 74, 108; magic-science conflicts of, 41–42; need of for integration, 131–132, 188–189; and perception of (a) clinic personnel, 132, 134, (b) physician

status, 148–149, 151, 158;
physicians' attitude toward
magic-science conflict of, 173;
status needs and clinic use of,
147, 187; tendency of to adopt
sick role, 82; traditional medical practice of, 41–42, 163,
164, 165

L

LAMPMAN, R. J., 64
Latent functions of medical institu-
tions, 3, 4, 5–6, 13–19, 195–
199; as catharsis, 13–15, 91–
109; and clinic use, 190–192;
as coping with failure, 15–16,
110–126; as integration into
society, 16, 127–143; as re-
solving magic-science conflict,
17–19, 161–178; as status
needs, 16–17, 144–160
LEE, S. S., 70n
LEES, D. S., 72n
LEVINE, G. N., 86
LEVY, M. J., JR., 182
LIEBERSON, S., 28
LIPSET, S. M., 144
LISSAK, M., 17
LOGAN, R. F. L., 64
LOGAN, W. P. D., 64, 70

M

MAC GREGOR, F. C., 94
Magic-science conflicts, 17–19, 20,
161–178; and clinic use, 167–
169, 177, 185–186, 189; among
Kurdish Jews, 41–42; in perception of physician, 163, 167,
171, 178, 185–186; physician's
response to, 169–176, 177–178;
testing hypothesis of, 165–169,
177
Malingerers, 112, 113, 118–119
MARTIN, J. P., 63
MASSRY, S., 72, 74, 75
MATRAS, J., 16, 17
MECHANIC, D., 20, 81, 82, 83n
Medical institution: catharsis function of, 13–15, 91–109; latent

functions of, 3, 4, 5–6, 13–19,
195–199; manifest functions
of, 3; motivation for use of,
3–4, 5; prestige of, 9. *See also*
Clinic use; Kupat Holim;
Latent functions of medical
institutions
Medical practices: social functions
of, 181–199; traditional, 138–
139, 140, 142–143, 163–164
Mellah, 43
MERTON, R. K., 3, 13, 17, 19, 183,
195, 197
MERTZ, J., 70
MIYAMOTO, S. F., 64
MOOALEM, F., 72, 74, 75
MORAG, P., 112, 136, 171
Moroccans, 4–5, 32, 56, 57; catharsis
needs of, 194–195; catharsis
needs of and nurse, 95–97,
106; clinic attendance of, 74,
118; date of immigration of,
34, 45–46, 47, 56; education
of, 43, 45; ethnographic sketch
of, 42–47; family structure of,
43; feeling of failure of, 114,
116; under French Protectorate, 44–47; integration needs
of, 131–132, 188–189; and
Moslems, 42–43; perception
of physician's status by, 148–
149; physicians' orientation to,
192–195; and physicians' response to (a) catharsis needs,
103–105, 107; (b) coping with
failure, 119–123, 125, (c)
magic-science conflict, 173–
176, 178, (d) status needs,
155–158, (e) traditional medical practices, 139, 140–141,
142–143; status needs of, 147;
tendency of to adopt sick role,
82, 83; and traditional medical practices, 43–44, 163, 164,
165; view of clinic personnel
by, 95, 132, 134
MORRIS, J. N., 164
MOSES, R., 11, 111, 112
Moshav (moshavim), 33

N

Near Eastern countries, immigrants from, 17, 26–27, 30
NEIMAN, I. S., 64
Non-Europeans: clinic use among, 73–74; vs. Europeans, socio-economic variables, 56–57; magic-science conflicts of, 17–19; perception of physician's status by, 148–151; physicians' prejudice against, 26–27, 29–30; tendency of to adopt sick role, 82, 86–87; view of clinic personnel by, 134, 136. *See also* Kurds; Moroccans
North African countries, immigrants from, 17, 26–27, 30
Nurse and catharsis needs of patient, 95–97, 99, 102, 106, 108, 109
NYMAN, K., 74

O

Outpatient clinic. *See* Clinic use

P

PARDESS, J., 72, 74, 75
PARSONS, T., 9, 10, 11, 24, 110
Patients' reports of clinic use, 69–72, 78
Petek, 11; ethnic variables in seeking, 114–117 125–126; importance of in feeling of failure, 112–117; physician and granting of, 118–123, 125–126
PHILLIPS, B. S., 70
Physician-patient relationship, 24–30
Physicians: and bureaucratic pressures, 27–28, 191–192; and catharsis needs of patient, 94–95, 97–100, 102, 103–109; and certification of illness, 11, 122–123, 125–126; and coping with failure, 118–123, 125–126; ethnic prejudices of, 26–27, 29–30, 37, 192–195; group membership of, 28; and integration into Israel, 136–141, 142–143; and magic-science conflict, 169–176, 177–178; and ma-

lingerers, 112, 113, 118–119; and norms of society, 26–27; and petek-granting, 11, 122–123, 125–126; Polish, 152, 158–159; role of, 11–13; Rumanian, 28, 152; sampling of for study, 34–35; and status needs of patients, 155–158, 159–160; status of, 144–145, 148–153, 158, 187–188; universalistic orientation of, 11–13, 127–128
Poles, 4–5, 32, 56, 57; date of immigration of, 55, 56; education of, 52; ethnographic sketch of, 50–55; family and communal life of, 51–52, 53–54; need of for integration, 131–132; perception of physicians' status by, 151–153, 158–159; persecution of, 51, 53–55; during post-World War II period, 54–55; during pre-World War II period, 50–53; status needs of, 187, 188; tendency of to adopt sick role, 83; and traditional medical practice, 163–164; during World War II, 53–54
POPON, C., 64
Prejudice: ethnic, of clinic personnel, 131–132, 192–195; against Near Easterners, 26–27, 30; against North Africans, 26–27, 30
PUROLA, T., 74

R

Research: on ethnic groups, 38–58; on Kupat Holim members, 31–34; on Kupat Holim physicians, 34–35; procedures of, 31–37; questionnaires for, 35–37; sampling in, 31–35
ROEMER, M. I., 14
ROSENSTOCK, I. M., 4, 81
ROSSI, P. H., 144
Rumanian physicians, 28

Rumanians, 4–5, 32, 56, 57, 194–195; catharsis needs of and (a) high clinic use, 108–109, (b) nurse, 99, 108–109, (c) physician, 95, 103–105, 107, 109; date of immigration of, 50, 56; education of, 48, 49; ethnographic sketch of, 47–50; need of for integration, 131–132; perception of physicians' status by, 151, 158; persecutions of, 48, 49, 50; physicians' orientations to, 192–195; and physicians' responses to (a) coping with failure, 119–123, 125, (b) magic-science conflicts, 173–176, 178, (c) status needs of, 155–158, (d) traditional medical practices of, 139, 140, 142–143; and traditional medical practice, 163, 164

S

SA'ADIA, H., 72, 73–74, 75
SANDERS, B. S., 70
SANDERS, I. Y., 91
SCHUMAN, H., 150
Science-magic conflicts. See Magic-science conflicts
SELIGSON-SINGER, S., 72, 72n
SHEATSLEY, P. B., 64
SHEPS, C. G., 70n
SHIPMAN, G. A., 64
SHOSTAK, A., 86
SHUVAL, J. T., 15, 16, 17, 26, 128
Sick role, 9–11, 19–23, 80–87; defining oneself in, 80–87; ethnic groups, adopting, 82–83, 86–87; legitimation of, 111–113; as means of coping with failure, 10, 15–16, 110–126; physicians' attitude toward, 25–26; rewards of, 81, 110–111, 112–113; tendency of Jews to adopt, 82–83; type of individual adopting, 19–23; variables among groups adopting, 82–87. See also Petek

SIEVERS, K., 74
SILVER, G. A., 73n
SIMMONS, O. G., 94, 106, 150
SIMMONS, W. R., 70n
SIMON, A. J., 5n
SINAI, N., 64
Social functions of medical practice, 181–199
SOLON, J. A., 70n
Status needs, 16–17, 144–160; and clinic use, 153–155, 159, 187–188, 189–190; comparison of those of ethnic groups, 147; and education, 145–147; physicians' response to, 155–158; and prestige of physician, 147–148, 153–155, 159; testing hypothesis of, 148–153
STEVENSON, J. S. K., 64
STOEKLE, J. D., 15n, 110
STREIB, G. F., 70
SUCHMAN, E. A., 70, 82, 130, 163
Superstition and magic among Kurdish Jews, 41–42
SZASZ, T. S., 24

T

TAYLOR, S., 64
TODD, J. W., 164
Traditional medical practices, 163–164. See also Magic-science conflicts
TRUSSELL, R. R., 70, 70n

U

United Nations Statistical Office, 64–65
U.S. National Health Survey, 70, 70n, 71
Utilization rate. See Clinic use

V

VACEK, M., 64
VARON, M., 72, 74, 75
VELDHOYZEN VAN ZANTEN, R. C., 64
VOLKART, E. A., 20, 81
VUKMANOVIC, C., 64

W

WAMOSCHER, Z., 74, 75

WEBER, A., 64

WEINBERG, A. A., 14

WEISKOPF, P., 72, 74, 75

WITTS, L. J., 164

World Health Organization, 61, 66–67

WULMAN, L., 53

Z

ZBOROWSKI, M., 9, 82, 144

ZOLA, I. K., 81, 110